Anonymous

The Whole Book of Psalms

In Metre with Hymns

Anonymous

The Whole Book of Psalms
In Metre with Hymns

ISBN/EAN: 9783337345846

Printed in Europe, USA, Canada, Australia, Japan

Cover: Foto ©Lupo / pixelio.de

More available books at **www.hansebooks.com**

THE
WHOLE BOOK
OF
PSALMS,
IN METRE;

WITH

HYMNS,

SUITED TO

THE FEASTS AND FASTS OF THE CHURCH,

AND

OTHER OCCASIONS

OF

PUBLIC WORSHIP.

NEW-YORK:

PRINTED BY H. GAINE, AT THE BIBLE, HANOVER-SQUARE,

M.DCC.XCIII.

BY the Bishops, the Clergy, and the Laity of the Protestant Episcopal Church in the United States of America, in Convention, this thirteenth day of October, in the year of our Lord one thousand seven hundred and eighty nine—

This Translation of the Whole Book of Psalms into Metre, with Hymns, is set forth, and allowed to be sung in all Congregations of the said Church, before and after Morning and Evening Prayer, and also before and after Sermons, at the discretion of the Minister.

And it shall be the duty of every Minister of any Church, either by standing directions, or from time to time, to appoint the Portions of Psalms which are to be sung.

And further, it shall be the duty of every Minister, with such assistance as he can obtain from persons skilled in music, to give order concerning the Tunes to be sung, at any time, in his Church: And, especially, it shall be his duty, to suppress all light and unseemly music; and all indecency and irreverence in the performance; by which, vain and ungodly persons profane the service of the Sanctuary.

The PSALMS of DAVID, in Metre.

PSALM I.

1 HOW bleſt is he, who ne'er conſents
 by ill advice to walk,
Nor ſtands in ſinners ways, nor ſits
 where men profanely talk;
2 But makes the perfect law of God
 his buſ'neſs and delight;
Devoutly reads therein by day,
 and meditates by night.
3 Like ſome fair tree, which, fed by ſtreams,
 with timely fruit does bend,
He ſtill ſhall flouriſh, and ſucceſs
 all his deſigns attend.
4 Ungodly men, and their attempts,
 no laſting root ſhall find;
Untimely blaſted, and diſpers'd
 like chaff before the wind.
5 Their guilt ſhall ſtrike the wicked dumb
 before their Judge's face:
No formal hypocrite ſhall then
 among the ſaints have place.
6 For God approves the juſt man's ways;
 to happineſs they tend:
But ſinners, and the paths they tread,
 ſhall both in ruin end.

PSALM II.

1 WITH reſtleſs and ungovern'd rage,
 why do the heathen ſtorm?
Why in ſuch raſh attempts engage,
 as they can ne'er perform?
2 The great in council and in might
 their various forces bring;
Againſt the Lord they all unite,
 and his anointed King.
3 " Muſt we ſubmit to their commands?"
 preſumptuouſly they ſay:
" No, let us break their ſlaviſh bands,
 " and caſt their chains away."
4 But God, who ſits enthron'd on high,
 and ſees how they combine,
Does their conſpiring ſtrength defy,
 and mocks their vain deſign.
5 Thick clouds of wrath divine ſhall break
 on his rebellious foes;
And thus will he in thunder ſpeak
 to all that dare oppoſe:

6 " Though madly you dispute my will,
  " the king that I ordain,
  " Whose throne is fix'd on Sion's hill,
  " shall there securely reign."

7 Attend, O earth, whilst I declare
  God's uncontroul'd decree:
  " Thou art my son; this day, my heir,
  " have I begotten thee.

8 " Ask, and receive thy full demands;
  " thine shall the heathen be;
  " The utmost limits of the lands
  " shall be possess'd by thee.

9 " Thy threat'ning sceptre thou shalt shake,
  " and crush them ev'ry where;
  " As massay bars of iron break
  " the potter's brittle ware."

10 Learn then, ye princes; and give ear,
  ye judges of the earth;

11 Worship the Lord with holy fear;
  rejoice with awful mirth.

12 Appease the Son with due respect,
  your timely homage pay:
  Lest he revenge the bold neglect,
  incens'd by your delay.

13 If but in part his anger rise,
  who can endure the flame?
  Then blest are they, whose hope relies
  on his most holy Name.

PSALM III.

1 HOW many, Lord, of late are grown
  the troublers of my peace!
  And as their numbers hourly rise,
  so does their rage increase.

2 Insulting, they my soul upbraid,
  and him whom I adore;
  " The God in whom he trusts," say they,
  " shall rescue him no more."

3 But thou, O Lord, art my defence;
  on thee my hopes rely;
  Thou art my glory, and shall yet
  lift up my head on high.

4 Since whensoe'er, in like distress,
  to God I made my pray'r,
  He heard me from his holy hill;
  why should I now despair?

5 Guarded by him, I laid me down
  my sweet repose to take;

For

PSALM IV.

For I through him securely sleep,
   through him in safety wake.
6 No force nor fury of my foes
   my courage shall confound,
Were they as many hosts as men,
   that have beset me round.
7 Arise, and save me, O my God,
   who oft hast own'd my cause,
And scatter'd oft these foes to me,
   and to thy righteous laws.
8 Salvation to the Lord belongs;
   he only can defend:
His blessing he extends to all
   that on his pow'r depend.

PSALM IV.

1 O Lord, that art my righteous Judge,
   to my complaint give ear:
Thou still redeem'st me from distress;
   have mercy, Lord, and hear.
2 How long will ye, O sons of men,
   to blot my fame devise?
How long your vain designs pursue,
   and spread malicious lies?
3 Consider that the righteous man
   is God's peculiar choice;
And when to him I make my pray'r,
   he always hears my voice.
4 Then stand in awe of his commands,
   flee ev'ry thing that's ill,
Commune in private with your hearts,
   and bend them to his will.
5 The place of other sacrifice
   let righteousness supply;
And let your hope, securely fix'd,
   on God alone rely.
6. While worldly minds impatient grow
   more prosp'rous times to see;
Still let the glories of thy face
   shine brightly, Lord, on me.
7 So shall my heart o'erflow with joy,
   more lasting and more true
Than theirs, who stores of corn and wine
   successively renew.
8 Then down in peace I'll lay my head,
   and take my needful rest;
No other guard, O Lord, I crave,
   of thy defence possess'd.

PSALM V.

1 LORD, hear the voice of my complaint,
   accept my secret pray'r;
2 To thee alone, my King, my God,
   will I for help repair.
3 Thou in the morn my voice shalt hear,
   and with the dawning day
   To thee devoutly I'll look up,
   to thee devoutly pray.
4 For thou the wrongs that I sustain
   canst never, Lord, approve,
   Who from thy sacred dwelling-place
   all evil dost remove.
5 Not long shall stubborn fools remain
   unpunish'd in thy view;
   All such as act unrighteous things
   thy vengeance shall pursue.
6 The sland'ring tongue, O God of truth,
   by thee shall be destroy'd,
   Who hat'st alike the man in blood
   and in deceit employ'd.
7 But when thy boundless grace shall me
   to thy lov'd courts restore,
   On thee I'll fix my longing eyes,
   and humbly there adore.
8 Conduct me by thy righteous laws,
   for watchful is my foe;
   Therefore, O Lord, make plain the way
   wherein I ought to go.
9 Their mouth vents nothing but deceit;
   their heart is set on wrong;
   Their throat is a devouring grave;
   they flatter with their tongue.
10 By their own counsels let them fall,
   oppress'd with loads of sin;
   For they against thy righteous laws
   have harden'd rebels been.
11 But let all those that trust in thee,
   with shouts their joy proclaim;
   Let them rejoice whom thou preserv'st,
   and all that love thy name.
12 To righteous men, the righteous Lord
   his blessing will extend;
   And with his favour all his saints,
   as with a shield, defend.

PSALM VI.

1 THY dreadful anger, Lord, restrain,
   and spare a wretch forlorn;

Correct

Correct me not in thy fierce wrath,
   too heavy to be borne.
2 Have mercy, Lord; for I grow faint,
   unable to endure
The anguish of my aching bones,
   which thou alone can'st cure.
3 My tortur'd flesh distracts my mind,
   and fills my soul with grief;
But, Lord, how long wilt thou delay
   to grant me thy relief?
4 Thy wonted goodness, Lord, repeat,
   and ease my troubled soul;
Lord, for thy wond'rous mercy's sake,
   vouchsafe to make me whole.
5 For after death no more can I
   thy glorious acts proclaim,
No pris'ners of the silent grave
   can magnify thy Name.
6 Quite tir'd with pain, with groaning faint,
   no hope of ease I see;
The night, that quiets common griefs,
   is spent in tears by me.
7 My beauty fades, my sight grows dim,
   my eyes with weakness close;
Old-age o'ertakes me, whilst I think
   on my insulting foes.
8 Depart, ye wicked; in my wrongs
   ye shall no more rejoice;
For God, I find, accepts my tears,
   and listens to my voice.
9, 10 He hears, and grants my humble pray'r;
   and they that wish my fall,
Shall blush and rage to see that God
   protects me from them all.

PSALM VII.

1 O Lord my God, since I have plac'd
      my trust alone in thee,
From all my persecutor's rage
   do thou deliver me.
2 To save me from my threat'ning foe,
   Lord interpose thy pow'r;
Lest, like a savage lion, he
   my helpless soul devour.
3, 4 If I am guilty, or did e'er
   against his peace combine;
Nay, if I had not spar'd his life,
   Who sought unjustly mine;

A 4

5 Let then to persecuting foes
    my soul become a prey;
  Let them to earth tread down my life,
    in dust my honor lay.
6 Arise, and let thine anger, Lord,
    in my defence engage;
  Exalt thyself above my foes,
    and their insulting rage:
  Awake, awake, in my behalf,
    the judgment to dispense,
  Which thou hast righteously ordain'd
    for injur'd innocence.
7 So to thy throne, adoring crowds
    shall still for justice fly:
  Oh! therefore for their sake, resume
    thy judgment-seat on high.
8 Impartial Judge of all the world,
    I trust my cause to thee;
  According to my just deserts,
    so let thy sentence be.
9 Let wicked arts and wicked men
    together be o'erthrown;
  But guard the just, thou God, to whom
    the hearts of both are known.
10, 11 God me protects, not only me,
    but all of upright heart;
  And daily lays up wrath for those
    who from his laws depart.
12 If they persist, he whets his sword,
    his bow stands ready bent;
13 Ev'n now, with swift destruction wing'd,
    his pointed shafts are sent.
14 The plots are fruitless which my foe
    unjustly did conceive;
15 The pit he digg'd for me, has prov'd
    his own untimely grave.
16 On his own head his spite returns,
    whilst I from harm am free;
  On him the violence is fall'n,
    which he design'd for me.
17 Therefore will I the righteous ways
    of providence proclaim;
  I'll sing the praise of God most high,
    and celebrate his Name.

PSALM VIII.

1 O Thou, to whom all creatures bow
    within this earthly frame,

Through

PSALM IX.

Through all the world how great art thou!
   how glorious is thy Name!
In heav'n thy wond'rous acts are sung,
   nor fully reckon'd there;
2 And yet thou mak'st the infant tongue
   thy boundless praise declare.
Through thee the weak confound the strong,
   and crush their haughty foes;
And so thou quell the wicked throng,
   that thee and thine oppose.

3 When Heav'n, thy beauteous work on high,
   employs my wond'ring sight;
The moon, that nightly rules the sky,
   with stars of feebler light.
4 What's man, say I, that, Lord, thou lov'st
   to keep him in thy mind?
Or what his offspring, that thou prov'st
   to them so wond'rous kind?
5 Him next in pow'r thou didst create
   to thy celestial train;
6 Ordain'd, with dignity and state,
   o'er all thy works to reign.
7 They jointly own his pow'rful sway;
   the beasts that prey or graze;
8 The bird that wings its airy way;
   the fish that cuts the seas.

9 O Thou, to whom all creatures bow
   within this earthly frame,
Through all the world how great art thou!
   how glorious is thy Name!

PSALM IX.

1 TO celebrate thy praise, O Lord,
   I will my heart prepare;
To all the list'ning world, thy works,
   thy wond'rous works declare.
2 The thought of them shall to my soul
   exalted pleasures bring;
Whilst to thy name, O thou Most High,
   triumphant praise I sing.
3 Thou mad'st my haughty foes to turn
   their backs in shameful flight:
Struck with thy presence, down they fell,
   they perish'd at thy sight.
4 Against insulting foes advanc'd,
   thou didst my cause maintain;
My right asserting from thy throne,
   where truth and justice reign.

5 The insolence of heathen pride
    thou hast reduc'd to shame;
  Their wicked offspring quite destroy'd,
    and blotted out their name.
6 Mistaken foes, your haughty threats
    are to a period come;
  Our city stands, which you design'd
    to make our common tomb.
7, 8 The Lord forever lives, who has
    his righteous throne prepar'd,
  Impartial justice to dispense,
    to punish or reward.
9 God is a constant sure defence
    against oppressing rage:
  As troubles rise, his needful aids
    in our behalf engage.
10 All those who have his goodness prov'd
    will in his truth confide;
  Whose mercy ne'er forsook the man
    that on his help rely'd.
11 Sing praises therefore to the Lord,
    from Sion, his abode;
  Proclaim his deeds, till all the world
    confess no other God.

PART II.

12 When he enquiry makes for blood,
    he'll call the poor to mind:
  The injur'd humble man's complaint
    relief from him shall find.
13 Take pity on my troubles, Lord,
    which spiteful foes create,
  Thou that hast rescu'd me so oft
    from death's devouring gate.
14 In Sion then I'll sing thy praise,
    to all that love thy name;
  And, with louds shouts of grateful joy,
    thy saving pow'r proclaim.
15 Deep in the pit they digg'd for me,
    the heathen pride is laid;
  Their guilty feet to their own snare
    are heedlessly betray'd.
16 Thus, by the just returns he makes,
    the mighty Lord is konwn;
  While wicked men by their own plots,
    are shamefully o'erthrown.
17 No single sinner shall escape,
    by privacy obscur'd;

Nor nation, from his just revenge,
  by numbers be secur'd.
18 His suff'ring saints, when most distress'd
  he ne'er forgets to aid;
Their expectations shall be crown'd,
  though for a time delay'd.
19 Arise, O Lord, assert thy pow'r,
  and let not man o'ercome;
Descend to judgment, and pronounce
  the guilty heathen's doom.
20 Strike terror through the nations round,
  till, by consenting fear,
They to each other, and themselves,
  but mortal men appear.

PSALM X.

1 THY presence why withdraw'st thou, Lord?
    why hid'st thou now thy face,
  When dismal times of deep distress,
    call for thy wonted grace?
2 The wicked, swell'd with lawless pride,
    have made the poor their prey;
  O let them fall by those designs
    which they for others lay.
3 For straight they triumph, if success
    their thriving crimes attend;
  And sordid wretches, whom God hates,
    perversely they commend.
4 To own a pow'r above themselves,
    their haughty pride disdains;
  And therefore in their stubborn mind
    no thought of God remains.
5 Oppressive methods they pursue,
    and all their foes they slight;
  Because thy judgments unobserv'd,
    are far above their sight.
6 They fondly think their prosp'rous state
    shall unmolested be;
  They think their vain designs shall thrive,
    from all misfortunes free.
7 Vain and deceitful is their speech,
    with curses fill'd, and lies;
  By which the mischief of their heart
    they study to disguise.
8 Near public roads they lie conceal'd,
    and all their art employ,
  The innocent and poor at once
    to rifle and destroy.

9 Not

PSALM XI.

9 Not lions, couching in their dens,
   surprise their heedless prey
With greater cunning, or express
   more savage rage, than they.
10 Sometimes they act the harmless man,
   and modest looks they wear;
That so deceiv'd, the poor may less
   their sudden onset fear.

PART II.

11 For God, they think, no notice takes
   of their unrighteous deeds;
He never minds the suff'ring poor,
   nor their oppression heeds.
12 But thou, O Lord, at length arise,
   stretch forth thy mighty arm;
And, by the greatness of thy pow'r,
   defend the poor from harm.
13 No longer let the wicked vaunt,
   and, proudly boasting, say,
"Tush, God regards not what we do;
"he never will repay."
14 But sure thou seest, and all their deeds
   impartially dost try;
The orphan, therefore, and the poor,
   on thee for aid rely.
15 Defenceless let the wicked fall,
   of all their strength bereft;
Confound, O God, their dark designs,
   till no remains are left.
16 Assert thy just dominion, Lord,
   which shall forever stand;
Thou who the heathen didst expel
   from this thy chosen land.
17 Thou hear'st the humble supplicants,
   that to thy throne repair;
Thou first prepar'st their hearts to pray,
   and then accept'st their pray'r.
18 Thou, in thy righteous judgment, weigh'st
   the fatherless and poor;
That so the tyrants of the earth
   may persecute no more.

PSALM XI.

1 SINCE I have plac'd my trust in God,
   a refuge always nigh,
Why should I, like a tim'rous bird,
   to distant mountains fly?
2 Behold, the wicked bend their bow,
   and ready fix their dart,

PSALM XII.

 Lurking in ambush to destroy
  the men of upright heart.
3 When once the firm assurance fails,
  which public faith imparts,
 'Tis time for innocence to fly
  from such deceitful arts.
4 The Lord hath both a temple here,
  and righteous throne above;
 Where he surveys the sons of men,
  and how their councils move.
5 If God the righteous, whom he loves,
  for trial does correct,
 What must the sons of violence,
  whom he abhors, expect?
6 Snares, fire, and brimstone, on their heads
  shall in one tempest show'r;
 This dreadful mixture his revenge
  into their cup shall pour.
7 The righteous Lord will righteous deeds
  with signal favour grace,
 And to the upright man disclose
  the brightness of his face.

PSALM XII.

1 SINCE godly men decay, O Lord,
  do thou my cause defend;
 For scarce these wretched times afford
  one just and faithful friend.
2 One neighbour now can scarce believe
  what t'other does impart;
 With flatt'ring lips they all deceive,
  and with a double heart.
3 But lips that with deceit abound
  can never prosper long;
 God's righteous vengeance will confound
  the proud blaspheming tongue.
4 In vain those foolish boasters say,
  " our tongues are sure our own;
 " With doubtful words we'll still betray,
  " and be controul'd by none."
5 For God, who hears the suff'ring poor,
  and their oppression knows,
 Will soon arise and give them rest,
  in spite of all their foes.
6 The word of God shall still abide,
  and void of falshood be,
 As is the silver, sev'n times try'd,
  from drossy mixture free.

7 The promise of his aiding grace
  shall reach its purpos'd end;
  His servants from this faithful race
  he ever shall defend.
8 Then shall the wicked be perplex'd,
  nor know which way to fly;
  When those whom they despis'd and vex'd,
  shall be advanc'd on high.

PSALM XIII.

1 HOW long wilt thou forget me, Lord?
    must I for ever mourn?
  How long wilt thou withdraw from me,
    Oh, never to return?
2 How long shall anxious thoughts my soul,
    and grief my heart oppress?
  How long my enemies insult,
    and I have no redress?
3 Oh! hear, and to my longing eyes
    restore thy wonted light,
  And suddenly, or I shall sleep
    in everlasting night.
4 Restore me, lest they proudly boast
    'twas their own strength o'ercame;
  Permit not them that vex my soul
    to triumph in my shame.
5 Since I have always plac'd my trust
    beneath thy mercy's wing,
  Thy saving health will come; and then
    my heart with joy shall spring.
6 Then shall my song, with praise infpir'd,
    to thee my God ascend;
  Who to thy servant in distress
    such bounty didst extend.

PSALM XIV.

1 SURE wicked fools must needs suppose,
    that God is nothing but a name;
  Corrupt and lewd their practice grows;
    no breast is warm'd with holy flame.
2 The Lord look'd down from Heav'n's high tow'r,
    and all the sons of men did view,
  To see if any own'd his pow'r;
    if any truth or justice knew.
3 But all, he saw, were gone aside,
    all were degen'rate grown and base;
  None took religion for their guide,
    not one of all the sinful race.
4 But can these workers of deceit
    be all so dull and senseless grown,

That

That they, like bread my people eat,
   and God's almighty pow'r difown?
5 How will they tremble then for fear,
   when his juft wrath fhall them o'ertake?
   For to the righteous God is near,
   And never will their caufe forfake.
6 Ill men, in vain, with fcorn expofe
   thofe methods which the good purfue;
   Since God a refuge is for thofe,
   whom his juft eyes with favour view.
7 Would he his faving pow'r employ
   to break his people's fervile band,
   Then fhouts of univerfal joy
   fhould loudly echo through the land.

PSALM XV.

1 LORD, who's the happy man that may
   to thy bleft courts repair,
   Not, ftranger-like, to vifit them,
   but to inhabit there?
2 'Tis he, whofe ev'ry thought and deed
   by rules of virtue moves;
   Whofe gen'rous tongue difdains to fpeak
   the thing his heart difproves.
3 Who never did a flander forge,
   his neighbour's fame to wound;
   Nor hearken to a falfe report,
   by malice whifper'd round.
4 Who vice, in all its pomp and pow'r,
   can treat with juft neglect;
   And piety, though cloath'd in rags,
   religioufly refpect.
5 Who to his plighted vows and truft
   has ever firmly ftood;
   And though he promife to his lofs,
   he makes his promife good.
6 Whofe foul in ufury difdains
   his treafure to employ;
   Whom no rewards can ever bribe
   the guiltlefs to deftroy.
7 The man, who by his fteady courfe
   has happinefs infur'd,
   When earth's foundation fhakes, fhall ftand,
   by Providence fecur'd.

PSALM XVI.

1 PROTECT me from my cruel foes,
   and fhield me, Lord, from harm;
   Becaufe my truft I ftill repofe
   on thy Almighty arm.

2 My soul all help but thine does slight,
   all gods but thee disown;
   Yet can no deeds of mine requite
   the goodness thou hast shown.
3 But those that strictly virtuous are,
   and love the thing that's right,
   To favour always, and prefer,
   shall be my chief delight.
4 How shall their sorrows be increas'd,
   who other gods adore;
   Their bloody off'rings I detest,
   their very names abhor.
5 My lot is fall'n in that blest land
   where God is truly known;
   He fills my cup with lib'ral hand,
   'tis he supports my throne.
6 In nature's most delightful scene
   my happy portion lies;
   The place of my appointed reign
   all other lands outvies.
7 Therefore my soul shall bless the Lord,
   whose precepts give me light;
   And private counsel still afford
   in sorrows dismal night.
8 I strive each action to approve
   to his all-seeing eye;
   No danger shall my hopes remove,
   because he still is nigh.
9 Therefore my heart all grief defies,
   my glory does rejoice;
   My flesh shall rest, in hope to rise,
   wak'd by his pow'rful voice.
10 Thou, Lord, when I resign my breath,
   my soul from hell shalt free;
   Nor let thy Holy One in death
   the least corruption see.
11 Thou shalt the paths of life display,
   which to thy presence lead;
   Where pleasures dwell without allay,
   and joys that never fade.

PSALM XVII.

1 TO my just plea and sad complaint
      attend, O righteous Lord;
   And to my pray'r, as 'tis unfeign'd,
   a gracious ear afford.
2 As in thy sight I am approv'd,
   so let my sentence be;

And

And with impartial eyes, O Lord,
  my upright dealing see.
3 For thou haſt ſearch'd my heart by day,
  and viſited by night;
  And, on the ſtricteſt trial, found
  its ſecret motions right.
  Nor ſhall thy juſtice, Lord, alone
  my heart's deſigns acquit;
  For I have purpos'd that my tongue
  ſhall no offence commit.
4 I know what wicked men would do,
  their ſafety to maintain;
  But me thy juſt and mild commands
  from bloody paths reſtrain.
5 That I may ſtill, in ſpite of wrongs,
  my innocence ſecure,
  O guide me in thy righteous ways,
  and make my footſteps ſure.
6 Since, heretofore, I ne'er in vain
  to thee my pray'r addreſs'd;
  O! now, my God, incline thine ear
  to this my juſt requeſt.
7 The wonders of thy truth and love
  in my defence engage;
  Thou, whoſe right hand preſerves thy ſaints
  From their oppreſſor's rage.

PART. II.

8, 9 O! keep me in thy tend'reſt care;
  thy ſhelt'ring wings ſtretch out,
  To guard me ſafe from ſavage foes,
  that compaſs me about:
10 O'ergrown with luxury, incloſ'd
  in their own fat they lie;
  And, with a proud blaſpheming mouth,
  both God and man defy.
11 Well may they boaſt, for they have now
  my paths encompaſs'd round;
  Their eyes at watch, their bodies bow'd,
  and couching on the ground;
12 In poſture of a lion ſet,
  when greedy of his prey;
  Or a young lion, when he lurks
  within a covert way.
13 Ariſe, O Lord, defeat their plots,
  their ſwelling rage controul;
  From wicked men, who are thy ſ
  deliver thou my ſoul:

B   14 From

14 From worldly men, thy sharpest scourge,
   whose portion's here below;
   Who, fill'd with earthly stores, aspire
   no other bliss to know.
15 Their race is num'rous, that partake
   their substance while they live;
   Their heirs survive, to whom they may
   the vast remainder give.
16 But I, in uprightness, thy face
   shall view without controul;
   And, waking, shall its image find
   reflected in my soul.

PSALM XVIII.

1, 2 NO change of time shall ever shock
     my firm affection, Lord, to thee;
   For thou hast always been my rock,
     a fort'ress and defence to me.
   Thou, my deliv'rer art, my God;
     my trust is in thy mighty pow'r;
   Thou art my shield from foes abroad,
     at home my safeguard and my tow'r.
3 To thee I will address my pray'r,
     to whom all praise we justly owe;
   So shall I, by thy watchful care,
     be guarded from my treach'rous foe.
4, 5 By floods of wicked men distress'd,
     with seas of sorrow compass'd round,
   With dire infernal pangs oppress'd,
     in death's unwieldy fetters bound;
6 To heav'n I made my mournful pray'r,
     to God address'd my humble moan;
   Who graciously inclin'd his ear,
     and heard me from his lofty throne.

PART II.

7 When God arose my part to take,
     the conscious earth was struck with fear;
   The hills did at his presence shake,
     nor could his dreadful fury bear.
8 Thick clouds of smoke dispers'd abroad,
     ensigns of wrath, before him came;
   Devouring fire around him glow'd,
     that coals were kindled at its flame.
9 He left the beauteous realms of light,
     whilst heav'n bow'd down its awful head;
   Beneath his feet substantial night
     was like a sable carpet spread.
10 The chariot of the King of kings,
     which active troops of angels drew,

On

On a strong tempest's rapid wings,
  with most amazing swiftness flew.
11, 12 Black watery mists and clouds conspir'd,
  with thickest shades his face to veil;
But at his brightness soon retir'd,
  And fell in show'rs of fire and hail.
13 Through Heav'ns wide arch a thund'ring peal,
  God's angry voice did loudly roar;
While earth's sad face with heaps of hail,
  and flakes of fire, was cover'd o'er.
14 His sharpen'd arrows round he threw,
  which made his scatter'd foes retreat;
Like darts his nimble light'nings flew,
  and quickly finish'd their defeat.
15 The deep its secret stores disclos'd;
  the world's foundations naked lay;
By his avenging wrath expos'd,
  which fiercely rag'd that dreadful day.

PART III.

16 The Lord did on my side engage;
  from Heav'n, his throne, my cause upheld;
And snatch'd me from the furious rage
  of threat'ning waves, that proudly swell'd.
17 God his resistless pow'r employ'd
  my strongest foes attempts to break;
Who else with ease had soon destroy'd
  the weak defence that I could make.
18 Their subtle rage had near prevail'd,
  when I distress'd and friendless lay;
But still, when other succours fail'd,
  God was my firm support and stay.
19 From dangers that inclos'd me round,
  he brought me forth, and set me free;
For some just cause his goodness found,
  that mov'd him to delight in me.
20 Because in me no guilt remains,
  God does his gracious help extend:
My hands are free from bloody stains;
  therefore the Lord is still my friend.
21, 22 For I his judgments keep in sight,
  in his just paths I always trod;
I never did his statutes slight,
  nor loosely wander'd from my God.
23, 24 But still my soul, sincere and pure,
  did ev'n from darling sins refrain;
His favours therefore yet endure,
  because thy heart and hands are clean.

PART

PSALM XVIII.
PART IV.

25, 26 Thou suit'st, O Lord, thy righteous ways
    to various paths of human-kind;
They who for mercy merit praise,
    with thee shall wond'rous mercy find.
Thou to the just shalt justice show;
    the pure thy purity shall see:
Such as perversely choose to go,
    shall meet with due returns from thee.

27, 28 That he the humble soul will save,
    and crush the haughty's boasted might,
In me the Lord an instance gave,
    whose darkness he has turn'd to light.

29 On his firm succour I rely'd,
    and did o'er num'rous foes prevail;
Nor fear'd, whilst he was on my side,
    the best-defended walls to scale.

30 For God's designs shall still succeed,
    his word will bear the utmost test;
He's a strong shield to all that need,
    and on his sure protection rest.

31 Who then deserves to be ador'd,
    but God, on whom my hopes depend?
Or who, except the mighty Lord,
    can with resistless pow'r defend?

PART V.

32, 33 'Tis God that girds my armour on,
    and all my just designs fulfils;
Through him my feet can swiftly run,
    and nimbly climb the steepest hills.

34 Lessons of war from him I take,
    and manly weapons learn to wield;
Strong bows of steel with ease I break,
    forc'd by my stronger arms to yield.

35 The buckler of his saving health
    protects me from assaulting foes;
His hand sustains me still; my wealth
    and greatness from his bounty flows.

36 My goings he enlarg'd abroad,
    till then to narrow paths confin'd;
And, when in slipp'ry ways I trod,
    the method of my steps design'd.

37 Through him I num'rous hosts defeat,
    and flying squadrons captive take;
Nor from my fierce pursuit retreat,
    till I a final conquest make.

38 Cover'd with wounds, in vain they try
    their vanquish'd heads again to rear;

PSALM XVIII.

  Spite of their boasted strength, they lie
   beneath my feet, and grovel there.
39 God, when fresh armies take the field,
   Recruits my strength, my courage warms;
  He makes my strong opposers yield,
   subdu'd by my prevailing arms.
40 Through him the necks of prostrate foes
   my conqu'ring feet in triumph press;
  Aided by him, I root out those,
   who hate and envy my success.
41 With loud complaints all friends they try'd;
   but none was able to defend;
  At length to God for help they cry'd;
   but God would no assistance lend.
42 Like flying dust, which winds pursue,
   their broken troops I scatter'd round;
  Their slaughter'd bodies forth I threw,
   like loathsome dirt, that clogs the ground.

PART VI.

43 Our factious tribes, at strife till now,
   by God's appointment me obey;
  The heathen to my sceptre bow,
   and foreign nations own my sway.
44 Remotest realms their homage send,
   when my successful name they hear;
  Strangers for my commands attend,
   charm'd with respect, or aw'd by fear.
45 All to my summons tamely yield,
   or soon in battle are dismay'd;
  For stronger holds they quit the field,
   and still in strongest holds afraid.
46 Let the eternal Lord be prais'd,
   the rock on whose defence I rest!
  To highest Heav'ns his Name be rais'd,
   who me with his salvation bless'd!
47 'Tis God that still supports my right;
   his just revenge my foes pursues;
  'Tis he, that, with resistless might,
   fierce nations to my yoke subdues.
48 My universal safeguard he!
   from whom my lasting honours flow;
  He made me great, and set me free
   from my remorseless bloody foe.
49 Therefore, to celebrate his fame,
   my grateful voice to Heav'n I'll raise;
  And nations, strangers to his Name,
   shall thus be taught to sing his praise:

50 "God to his king deliv'rance sends;
   "shows his anointed signal grace;
   "His mercy evermore extends
   "to David, and his promis'd race."

PSALM XIX.

1 THE Heav'ns declare thy glory, Lord,
    which that alone can fill;
  The firmament and stars express
    their great Creator's skill.
2 The dawn of each returning day
    fresh beams of knowledge brings;
  And from the dark returns of night
    divine instruction springs.
3 Their pow'rful language to no realm
    or region is confin'd;
  'Tis nature's voice, and understood
    alike by all mankind.
4 Their doctrine does its sacred sense
    through earth's extent display;
  Whose bright contents the circling sun
    does round the world convey.
5 No bridegroom on his nuptial day,
    has such a chearful face;
  No giant does like him rejoice
    to run his glorious race.
6 From east to west, from west to east,
    his restless course he goes;
  And, through his progress, chearful light
    and vital warmth bestows.

PART II.

7 God's perfect law converts the soul;
    reclaims from false desires;
  With sacred wisdom his sure word
    the ignorant inspires.
8 The statutes of the Lord are just,
    and bring sincere delight;
  His pure commands in search of truth
    assist the feeblest sight.
9 His perfect worship here is fix'd,
    on sure foundations laid;
  His equal laws are in the scales
    of truth and justice weigh'd;
10 Of more esteem than golden mines,
    of gold refin'd with skill;
  More sweet than honey, or the drops
    that from the comb distil.
11 My trusty counsellors they are,
    and friendly warnings give;

Divine

Divine rewards attend on those,
    who by thy precepts live.
12 But what frail man observes how oft
    he does from virtue fall?
  O cleanse me from my secret faults,
    thou God that know'st them all!
13 Let no presumptuous sin, O Lord,
    dominion have o'er me;
  That, by thy grace preserv'd, I may
    the great transgression flee.
14 So shall my pray'r and praises be
    with thy acceptance blest;
  And I secure on thy defence,
    my Strength and Saviour, rest.

PSALM XX.

1 THE Lord to thy request attend,
    and hear thee in distress;
  The name of Jacob's God defend,
    and grant thy arms success:
2 To aid thee from on high repair,
    and strength from Sion give;
3 Remember all thy off'rings there,
    thy sacrifice receive:
4 To compass thy own heart's desire
    thy counsels still direct;
  Make kindly all events conspire
    to bring them to effect.
5 To thy salvation, Lord, for aid
    we chearfully repair,
  With banners in thy name display'd;
    " The Lord accept thy pray'r."
6 Our hopes are fix'd, that now the Lord
    our sov'reign will defend;
  From Heav'n resistless aid afford,
    and to his pray'r attend.
7 Some trust in steeds for war design'd;
    on chariots some rely;
  Against them all we'll call to mind
    the power of God most high.
8 But from their steeds and chariots thrown,
    behold them through the plain,
  Disorder'd, broke, and trampled down,
    whilst firm our troops remain.
9 Still save us, Lord, and still proceed
    our rightful cause to bless;
  Hear, King of Heav'n, in times of need,
    the pray'rs that we address.

PSALM XXI.

1 THE king, O Lord, with songs of praise,
    shall in thy strength rejoice;
With thy salvation crown'd, shall raise
    to Heaven his chearful voice.
2 For thou, whate'er his lips request,
    not only dost impart;
But hast, with thy acceptance, blest
    the wishes of his heart.
3 Thy goodness and thy tender care
    have all his hopes outgone;
A crown of gold thou mad'st him wear,
    and sett'st it firmly on.
4 He pray'd for life; and thou, O Lord,
    did'st to his prayer attend,
And graciously to him afford
    a life that ne'er shall end.
5 Thy sure defence through nations round
    has spread his glorious name:
And his successful actions crown'd
    with majesty and fame.
6 Eternal blessings thou bestow'st,
    and mak'st his joys increase;
Whilst thou to him unclouded show'st
    the brightness of thy face.

PART II.

7 Because the king on God alone
    for timely aid relies;
His mercy still supports his throne,
    and all his wants supplies.
8 But, righteous Lord, thy stubborn foes
    shall feel thy heavy hand;
Thy vengeful arm shall find out those,
    that hate thy mild command.
9 When thou against them dost engage,
    thy just but dreadful doom
Shall, like a glowing oven's rage,
    their hopes and them consume.
10 Nor shall thy furious anger cease,
    or with their ruin end;
But root out all their guilty race,
    and to their seed extend.
11 For all their thoughts were set on ill,
    their hearts on malice bent;
But thou with watchful care didst still
    the ill effects prevent.
12 While they their swift retreat shall make
    to 'scape thy dreadful might,

Thy

PSALM XXII.

Thy swifter arrows shall o'ertake,
   and gall them in their flight.
13 Thus, Lord, thy wond'rous strength disclose,
   and thus exalt thy fame;
Whilst we glad songs of praise compose
   to thy Almighty Name.

PSALM XXII.

1 MY God, my God, why leav'st thou me
   when I with anguish faint?
O! why so far from me remov'd,
   and from my loud complaint?
2 All day, but all the day unheard,
   to thee do I complain;
With cries implore relief all night,
   but cry all night in vain.
3 Yet thou art still the righteous Judge
   of innocence oppress'd;
And therefore Israel's praises are
   of right to thee address'd.
4, 5 On thee our ancestors rely'd,
   and thy deliverance found;
With pious confidence they pray'd,
   and with success were crown'd.
6 But I am treated like a worm;
   like none of human birth;
Not only by the great revil'd,
   but made the rabble's mirth.
7 With laughter all the gazing crowd
   my agonies survey;
They shoot the lip, they shake the head,
   and thus deriding say;
8 " In God he trusted, boasting oft
   " that he was Heav'n's delight;
" Let God come down to save him now,
   " and own his favourite."

PART II.

9 Thou mad'st my teeming mother's womb
   a living offspring bear;
When but a suckling at the breast,
   I was thy early care.
10 Thou, guardian like, didst shield from wrongs
   my helpless infant days;
And since hast been my God, and guide
   through life's bewilder'd ways.
11 Withdraw not then so far from me,
   when trouble is so nigh;
O, send me help! thy help, on which
   I only can rely.

12 High pamper'd bulls, a frowning herd,
   from Bafan's foreft met,
   With ftrength proportion'd to their rage,
   have me around befet.
13 They gape on me, and ev'ry mouth
   a yawning grave appears;
   The defert lion's favage roar
   lefs dreadful is than theirs.

PART III.

14 My blood like water's fpill'd, my joints
   are rack'd and out of frame;
   My heart diffolves within my breaft,
   like wax before the flame.
15 My ftrength like potter's earth, is parch'd;
   my tongue cleaves to my jaws;
   And to the filent fhades of death
   my fainting foul withdraws.
16 Like blood-hounds, to furround me, they
   in pack'd affemblies meet:
   They pierc'd my innofenfive hands;
   they pierc'd my harmlefs feet.
17 My body's rack'd, till all my bones
   diftinctly may be told;
   Yet fuch a fpectacle of woe
   as paftime they behold.
18 As fpoil, my garments they divide,
   lots for my vefture caft;
19 Therefore approach, O Lord, my ftrength,
   'and to my fuccour hafte.
20 From their fharp fwords protect thou me;
   of all but life bereft:
   Nor let my darling in the pow'r
   of cruel dogs be left.
21 To fave me from the lion's jaws,
   thy prefent fuccour fend;
   As once, from goring unicorns,
   thou didft my life defend.
22 Then to my brethren I'll declare
   the triumphs of thy Name;
   In prefence of affembled faints
   thy glory thus proclaim:
23 " Ye worfhippers of Jacob's God,
   " all you of Ifrael's line,
   " O praife the Lord, and to your praife
   " fincere obedience join.
24 " He ne'er difdain'd on low diftrefs
   "to caft a gracious eye;
   " Nor turn'd from poverty his face,
   " but hears its humble cry."

PSALM XXIII.
PART IV.

25 Thus, in thy sacred courts, will I
my chearful thanks express;
In presence of thy saints perform
the vows of my distress.
26 The meek companions of my grief
shall find my table spread;
And all that seek the Lord, shall be
with joys immortal fed.
27 Then shall the glad converted world
to God their homage pay;
And scatter'd nations of the earth
one Sov'reign Lord obey.
28 'Tis his supreme prerogative
o'er subject kings to reign;
'Tis just that he should rule the world,
who does the world sustain.
29 The rich, who are with plenty fed,
his bounty must confess;
The sons of want, by him reliev'd,
their gen'rous Patron bless.
 With humble worship to his throne
they all for aid resort;
That pow'r, which first their beings gave,
can only them support.
30, 31 Then shall a chosen spotless race,
devoted to his Name,
To their admiring heirs his truth,
and glorious acts, proclaim.

PSALM XXIII.

1 THE Lord himself, the mighty Lord,
vouchsafes to be my Guide;
The Shepherd, by whose constant care,
my wants are all supply'd.
2 In tender grass he makes me feed,
and gently there repose;
Then leads me to cool shades, and where
refreshing water flows.
3 He does my wand'ring soul reclaim,
and, to his endless praise,
Instruct with humble zeal to walk
in his most righteous ways.
4 I pass the gloomy vale of death,
from fear and danger free;
For there his aiding rod and staff
defend and comfort me.
5 In presence of my spiteful foes
he does my table spread;

He crowns my cup with chearful wine,
    with oil anoints my head.
6 Since God doth thus his wond'rous love
    through all my life extend,
That life to him I will devote,
    and in his temple spend.

PSALM XXIV.

1 THE spacious earth is all the Lord's,
    the Lord's her fulness is;
The world, and they that dwell therein,
    by sov'reign right are his.
2 He fram'd and fix'd it on the seas;
    and his Almighty hand,
Upon inconstant floods, has made
    the stable fabric stand.
3 But for himself, this Lord of all
    one chosen seat design'd;
O! who shall to that sacred hill
    deserv'd admittance find?
4 The man, whose hands and heart are pure,
    whose thoughts from pride are free;
Who honest poverty prefers
    to gainful perjury.
5 This, this is he, on whom the Lord
    shall show'r his blessings down;
Whom God, his Saviour, shall vouchsafe
    with righteousness to crown.
6 Such is the race of saints, by whom
    the sacred courts are trod;
And such the proselytes that seek
    the face of Jacob's God.
7 Erect your heads, eternal gates;
    unfold, to entertain
The King of Glory: see! he comes
    with his celestial train.
8 Who is the King of Glory? who?
    the Lord, for strength renown'd;
In battle mighty; o'er his foes
    eternal victor crown'd.
9 Erect your heads, ye gates; unfold
    in state to entertain
The King of Glory: see! he comes
    with all his shining train.
10 Who is the King of Glory? who?
    the Lord of hosts renown'd;
Of glory he alone is King,
    who is with glory crown'd.

PSALM XXV.

1, 2 TO God, in whom I truſt,
       I lift my heart and voice ;
O ! let me not be put to ſhame,
    nor let my foes rejoice.
3 Thoſe who on thee rely,
    let no diſgrace attend ;
Be that the ſhameful lot of ſuch,
    as wilfully offend.
4, 5 To me thy truth impart,
    and lead me in thy way ;
For thou art he that brings me help ;
    on thee I wait all day.
6 Thy mercies, and thy love,
    O Lord, recall to mind ;
And graciouſly continue ſtill,
    as thou wert ever, kind.
7 Let all my youthful crimes
    be blotted out by thee ;
And, for thy wond'rous goodneſs ſake,
    in mercy think on me,
8 His mercy, and his truth,
    the righteous Lord diſplays,
In bringing wand'ring ſinners home,
    and teaching them his ways.
9 He thoſe in juſtice guides,
    who his direction ſeek ;
And in his ſacred paths ſhall lead
    the humble and the meek.
10 Through all the ways of God
    both truth and mercy ſhine,
To ſuch as, with religious hearts,
    to his bleſt will incline.

PART II.

11 Since mercy is the grace,
    that moſt exalts thy fame,
Forgive my heinous ſin, O Lord,
    and ſo advance thy Name.
12 Who'er, with humble fear,
    to God his duty pays,
Shall find the Lord a faithful guide,
    in all his righteous ways.
13 His quiet ſoul with peace
    ſhall be for ever bleſs'd ;
And by his num'rous race the land
    ſucceſſively poſſeſs'd.
14 For God to all his ſaints
    his ſecret will imparts,

And

PSALM XXVI.

And does his gracious cov'nant write
   in their obedient hearts.
15 To him I lift my eyes,
   and wait his timely aid,
Who breaks the ſtrong and treach'rous ſnare,
   which for my feet was laid.
16 O! turn, and all my griefs,
   in mercy, Lord, redreſs;
For I am compaſs'd round with woes,
   and plung'd in deep diſtreſs.
17 The ſorrows of my heart
   to mighty ſums increaſe;
O! from this dark and diſmal ſtate
   my troubled ſoul releaſe!
18 Do thou, with tender eyes,
   my ſad affliction ſee;
Acquit me, Lord, and from my guilt
   entirely ſet me free.
19 Conſider, Lord, my foes,
   how vaſt their numbers grow,
What lawleſs force and rage they uſe,
   what boundleſs hate they ſhow.
20 Protect, and ſet my ſoul
   from their fierce malice free;
Nor let me be aſham'd, who place
   my ſtedfaſt truſt in thee.
21 Let all my righteous acts
   to full perfection riſe:
Becauſe my firm and conſtant hope
   on thee alone relies.
22 To Iſrael's choſen race
   continue ever kind;
And, in the midſt of all their wants,
   let them thy ſuccour find.

PSALM XXVI.

1 JUDGE me, O Lord, for I the paths
   of righteouſneſs have trod;
I cannot fail, who all my truſt
   repoſe on thee, my God.
2, 3 Search thou my heart, whoſe innocence
   will ſhine the more 'tis try'd;
For I have kept thy grace in view,
   and made thy truth my guide.
4 I never for companions took
   the idle or profane;
No hypocrite, with all his arts,
   could e'er my friendſhip gain.
5 I hate the buſy plotting crew,
   who make diſtracted times;

And

PSALM XXVII.

 And shun their wicked company,
  as I avoid their crimes.
6 I'll wash my hands in innocence,
  and bring a heart so pure,
 That, when thy altar I approach,
  my welcome shall secure.
7, 8 My thanks I'll publish there, and tell
  how thy renown excels;
 That seat affords me most delight,
  in which thy honour dwells.
9 Pass not on me the sinners' doom,
  who murder make their trade;
10 Who others' rights, by secret bribes,
  of open force, invade.
11 But I will walk in paths of truth,
  and innocence pursue;
 Protect me, therefore, and to me
  thy mercies, Lord, renew.
12 In spite of all assaulting foes,
  I still maintain my ground;
 And shall survive among thy saints,
  thy praises to resound.

PSALM XXVII.

1 WHOM should I fear, since God to me
  is saving health and light?
 Since strongly he my life supports,
  what can my soul affright?
2 With fierce intent my flesh to tear,
  when foes beset me round,
 They stumbled, and their haughty crests
  were made to strike the ground.
3 Through him my heart, undaunted, dares
  with mighty hosts to cope;
 Through him, in doubtful straits of war,
  for good success I hope.
4 Henceforth, within his house to dwell
  I earnestly desire;
 His wond'rous beauty there to view,
  and of his will enquire.
5 For there I may with comfort rest,
  in times of deep distress;
 And safe, as on a rock, abide
  in that secure recess:
6 Whilst God o'er all my haughty foes
  my lofty head shall raise;
 And I my joyful tribute bring,
  with grateful songs of praise.

PART

PSALM XXVIII.
PART II.

7 Continue, Lord, to hear my voice,
  whenc'er to thee I cry;
  In mercy my complaints receive,
  nor my requeſt deny.

8 When us to ſeek thy glorious face
  thou kindly doſt advife;
  "Thy glorious face I'll always ſeek,"
  my grateful heart replies.

9 Then hide not thou thy face, O Lord,
  nor me in wrath reject;
  My God and Saviour, leave not him
  thou didſt ſo oft protect.

10 Though all my friends, and kindred too,
   their helpleſs charge forſake;
   Yet thou, whoſe love excels them all,
   wilt care and pity take.

11 Inſtruct me in thy paths, O Lord;
   my ways directly guide;
   Leſt envious men, who watch my ſteps,
   ſhould ſee me tread aſide.

12 Lord diſappoint my cruel foes;
   defeat their ill deſire,
   Whoſe lying lips, and bloody hands,
   againſt my peace conſpire.

13 I truſted that my future life
   ſhould with thy love be crown'd;
   Or elſe my fainting ſoul had ſunk,
   with ſorrow compaſs'd round.

14 God's time with patient faith expect,
   who will inſpire thy breaſt
   With inward ſtrength: do thou thy part,
   and leave to him the reſt.

PSALM XXVIII.

1 O Lord, my rock, to thee I cry,
   in ſighs conſume my breath;
  O! anſwer, or I ſhall become
   like thoſe that ſleep in death.

2 Regard my ſupplication, Lord,
   the cries that I repeat,
  With weeping eyes, and lifted hands,
   before thy mercy-ſeat.

3 Let me eſcape the ſinners' doom,
   who make a trade of ill,
  And ever ſpeak the perſon fair,
   whoſe blood they mean to ſpill.

4 According to their crimes' extent,
   let juſtice have its courſe;

  Relentless be to them, as they
   have sinn'd without remorse.
5 Since they the works of God despise,
   nor will his grace adore;
  His wrath shall utterly destroy,
   and build them up no more.
6 But I, with due acknowledgment,
   his praises will resound,
  From whom the cries of my distress
   a gracious answer found.
7 My heart its confidence repos'd
   in God, my strength and shield;
  In him I trusted, and return'd
   triumphant from the field.
  As he hath made my joys complete,
   'tis just that I should raise
  The chearful tribute of my thanks,
   and thus resound his praise:
8 " His aiding pow'r supports the troops,
  " that my just cause maintain:
  " 'Twas he advanc'd me to the throne;
  " 'tis he secures my reign."
9 Preserve thy chosen, and proceed
   thine heritage to bless;
  With plenty prosper them, in peace;
   in battle, with success.

PSALM XXIX.

1 YE princes, that in might excel,
   your grateful sacrifice prepare;
  God's glorious actions loudly tell,
   his wond'rous pow'r to all declare.
2 To his great name fresh altars raise;
   devoutly due respect afford;
  Him in his holy temple praise,
   where he's with solemn state ador'd.
3 'Tis he that, with amazing noise,
   the wat'ry clouds in sunder breaks;
  The ocean trembles at his voice,
   when he from heav'n in thunder speaks.
4, 5 How full of pow'r his voice appears!
   with what majestic terror crown'd!
  Which from their roots tall cedars tears,
   and strows their scatter'd branches round.
6 They, and the hills on which they grow,
   are sometimes hurry'd far away;
  And leap, like hinds that bounding go,
   or unicorns in youthful play.

7, 8 When

PSALM XXX.

7, 8 When God in thunder loudly speaks,
    and scatter'd flames of light'ning sends,
The forest nods, the desert quakes,
    and stubborn Kadesh lowly bends.
9 He makes the hinds to cast their young,
    and lays the beasts' dark coverts bare;
While those that to his courts belong,
    securely sing his praises there.
10, 11 God rules the angry floods on high;
    his boundless sway shall never cease;
His saints with strength he will supply,
    and bless his own with constant peace.

PSALM XXX.

1 I'LL celebrate thy praises, Lord,
    who didst thy pow'r employ
To raise my drooping head, and check
    my foes' insulting joy.
2, 3 In my distress I cry'd to thee,
    who kindly didst relieve,
And from the grave's expecting jaws
    my hopeless life retrieve.
4 Thus to his courts ye saints of his,
    with songs of praise repair;
With me commemorate his truth,
    and providential care.
5 His wrath has but a moment's reign,
    his favour no decay;
Y... night of grief is recompens'd
    with joys returning day.
6 But I, in prosp'rous days presum'd;
    no sudden change I fear'd;
Whilst in my sunshine of success
    no low'ring cloud appear'd.
7 But soon I found thy favour, Lord,
    my empire's only trust;
For when thou hidd'st thy face, I saw
    my honour laid in dust.
8 Then as I vainly had presum'd
    my error I confess'd;
And thus with supplicating voice,
    thy mercy's throne addrefs'd:
9 " What profit is there in my blood,
    " congeal'd by death's cold night?
" Can silent ashes speak thy praise,
    " thy wond'rous truth recite?
10 " Hear me, O Lord; in mercy hear;
    " thy wonted aid extend;

PSALM XXXI.

"Do thou send help, on whom alone
"I can for help depend."
11 'Tis done! thou haſt my mournful ſcene
to ſongs and dances turn'd;
Inveſted me with robes of ſtate,
who late in ſackcloth mourn'd.
12 Exalted thus, I'll gladly ſing
thy praiſe in grateful verſe;
And, as thy favours endleſs are,
thy endleſs praiſe rehearſe.

PSALM XXXI.

1 DEFEND me, Lord, from ſhame,
for ſtill I truſt in thee;
As juſt and righteous is thy Name,
from danger ſet me free.
2 Bow down thy gracious ear,
and ſpeedy ſuccour ſend;
Do thou my ſtedfaſt rock appear,
to ſhelter and defend.
3 Since thou, when foes oppreſs,
my rock and fortreſs art,
To guide me forth from this diſtreſs,
thy wonted help impart.
4 Releaſe me from the ſnare,
which they have cloſely laid;
Since I, O God, my ſtrength, repair
to thee alone for aid.
5 To thee, the God of truth,
my life, and all that's mine.
(For thou preſerv'dſt me from my youth,)
I willingly reſign.
6 All vain deſigns I hate
of thoſe that truſt in lies;
And ſtill my ſoul, in every ſtate,
to God for ſuccour flies.

PART II.

7 Thoſe mercies thou haſt ſhown,
I'll chearfully expreſs;
For thou haſt ſeen my ſtraits, and known
my ſoul in deep diſtreſs.
8 When Keilah's treach'rous race
did all my ſtrength incloſe,
Thou gav'ſt my feet a larger ſpace,
to ſhun my watchful foes.
9 Thy mercy, Lord, diſplay,
and hear my juſt complaint;
For both my ſoul and fleſh decay,
with grief and hunger faint.

C 2   10 Sad

PSALM XXXI.

10 Sad thoughts my life oppress;
    my years are spent in groans;
  My sins have made my strength decrease,
    and ev'n consum'd my bones.
11 My foes my suff'rings mock'd;
    my neighbours did upbraid;
  My friends, at sight of me, were shock'd,
    and fled, as men dismay'd.
12 Forsook by all am I,
    as dead, and out of mind;
  And like a shatter'd vessel lie,
    whose parts can ne'er be join'd.
13 Yet sland'rous words they speak,
    and seem my pow'r to dread;
  Whilst they together counsel take,
    my guiltless blood to shed.
14 But still my stedfast trust
    I on thy help repose ↄ
  That thou, my God, art good and just,
    my soul with comfort knows.

PART III.

15 Whate'er events betide,
    thy wisdom times them all;
  Then, Lord, thy servant safely hide
    from those that seek his fall.
16 The brightness of thy face
    to me, O Lord, disclose;
  And, as thy mercies still increase,
    preserve me 'from my foes.
17 Me from dishonour save,
    who still have call'd on thee;
  Let that, and silence in the grave,
    the sinner's portion be.
18 Do thou their tongues restrain,
    whose breath in lies is spent;
  Who false reports, with proud disdain,
    against the righteous vent.
19 How great thy mercies are
    to such as fear thy Name,
  Which thou for those that trust thy care,
    dost to the world proclaim!
20 Thou keep'st them in thy sight,
    from proud oppressors free;
  From tongues that do in strife delight.
    they are preserv'd by thee.
21 With glory and renown
    God's name be ever bless'd:

PSALM XXXII.

 Whose love, in Keilah's well-fenc'd town,
  was wond'rously express'd!
22 I said, in hasty flight,
  " I'm banish'd from thine eyes;"
 Yet still thou keep'st me in thy sight,
  and heard'st my earnest cries.
23 O! all ye saints, the Lord
  with eager love pursue;
 Who to the just will help afford,
  and give the proud their due.
24 Ye that on God rely,
  courageously proceed;
 For he will still your hearts supply
  with strength, in time of need.

PSALM XXXII.

1 HE's blest whose sins have pardon gain'd,
  no more in judgment to appear;
2 Whose guilt remission has obtain'd,
  and whose repentance is sincere.
3 While I conceal'd the fretting sore,
  my bones consum'd without relief;
 All day did I with anguish roar;
  but no complaints asswag'd my grief.
4 Heavy on me thy hand remain'd,
  by day and night alike distress'd,
 'Till quite of vital moisture drain'd,
  like land with summer's drought oppress'd.
5 No sooner I my wound disclos'd,
  the guilt that tortur'd me within,
 But thy forgiveness interpos'd,
  and mercy's healing balm pour'd in.
6 True penitents shall thus succeed,
  who seek thee whilst thou may'st be found;
 And, from the common deluge freed,
  shall see remorseless sinners drown'd.
7 Thy favour, Lord, in all distress,
  my tow'r of refuge I must own;
 Thou shalt my haughty foes suppress,
  and me with songs of triumph crown.
8 In my instruction then confide,
  ye that would truth's safe path descry;
 Your progress I'll securely guide,
  and keep you in my watchful eye.
9 Submit yourselves to wisdom's rule,
  like men that reason have attain'd;
 Not like th' ungovern'd horse and mule,
  whose fury must be curb'd and rein'd.

10 Sorrows on sorrows multiply'd,
   the harden'd sinner shall confound;
But them who in his truth confide,
   blessings of mercy shall surround.
11 His saints, that have perform'd his laws,
   their life in triumph shall employ;
Let them, as they alone have cause,
   in grateful raptures shout for joy.

PSALM XXXIII.

1 LET all the just to God, with joy,
      their chearful voices raise;
For well the righteous it becomes
   to sing glad songs of praise.
2, 3 Let harps, and psalteries, and lutes,
   in joyful concert meet;
And new-made songs of loud applause
   the harmony complete.
4, 5 For faithful is the word of God;
   his works with truth abound;
He justice loves; and all the earth
   is with his goodness crown'd.
6 By his Almighty Word, at first,
   the heav'nly arch was rear'd;
And all the beauteous hosts of light
   at his command appear'd.
7 The swelling floods, together roll'd,
   he makes in heaps to lie;
And lays, as in a store-house safe,
   the wat'ry treasures by.
8, 9 Let earth, and all that dwell therein,
   before him trembling stand;
For, when he spake the word, 'twas made;
   'twas fix'd at his command.
10 He, when the heathen closely plot,
   their councils undermines;
His wisdom ineffectual makes
   the peoples' rash designs.
11 Whate'er the mighty Lord decrees
   shall stand for ever sure;
The settled purpose of his heart
   to ages shall endure.

PART II.

12 How happy then are they, to whom
   the Lord for God is known!
Whom he, from all the world besides,
   has chosen for his own.
13, 14, 15 He all the nations of the earth,
   from heav'n, his throne, survey'd;

PSALM XXXIV.

He faw their works, and view'd their thoughts;
    by him their hearts were made.
16, 17 No king is fafe by num'rous hofts;
    their ftrength the ftrong deceives:
No manag'd horfe, by force or fpeed,
    his warlike rider faves.
18, 19 'Tis God, who thofe that truft in him
    beholds with gracious eyes;
He frees their foul from death; their want,
    in time of dearth, fupplies.
20, 21 Our foul on God with patience waits;
    our help and fhield is he;
Then, Lord, let ftill our hearts rejoice,
    becaufe we truft in thee.
22 The riches of thy mercy, Lord,
    do thou to us extend;
Since we, for all we want or wifh,
    on thee alone depend.

PSALM XXXIV.

1 THrough all the changing fcenes of life,
    in trouble and in joy,
The praifes of my God fhall ftill
    my heart and tongue employ.
2 Of his deliv'rance I will boaft,
    till all that are diftreft,
From my example comfort take,
    and charm their griefs to reft.
3 O! magnify the Lord with me,
    with me exalt his name:
4 When in diftrefs to him I call'd,
    he to my refcue came.
5 Their drooping hearts were foon refrefh'd,
    who look'd to him for aid;
Defir'd fuccefs in ev'ry face
    a chearful air difplay'd.
6 " Behold," fay they " behold the man,
    " whom providence reliev'd;
    " The man fo dang'roufly befet,
    " fo wond'roufly retriev'd!"
7 The hofts of God encamp around
    the dwellings of the juft;
Deliv'rance he affords to all
    who on his fuccour truft.
8 O! make but trial of his love,
    experience will decide
How bleft they are, and only they,
    who in his truth confide.

9 Fear him, ye saints; and you will then
 have nothing elſe to fear:
 Make you his ſervice your delight,
 your wants ſhall be his care.
10 While hungry lions lack their prey,
 the Lord will food provide
 For ſuch as put their truſt in him,
 and ſee their needs ſupply'd.

PART II.

11 Approach, ye piouſly diſpos'd,
 and my inſtruction hear;
 I'll teach you the true diſcipline
 of his religious fear.
12 Let him who length of life deſires,
 and proſp'rous days would ſee,
13 From ſland'ring language keep his tongue,
 his lips from falſhood free;
14 The crooked paths of vice decline,
 and virtue's ways purſue;
 Eſtabliſh peace, where 'tis begun;
 and where 'tis loſt, renew.
15 The Lord from heav'n beholds the juſt
 with favourable eyes;
 And, when diſtreſs'd, his gracious ear
 is open to their cries;
16 But turns his wrathful look on thoſe,
 whom mercy can't reclaim,
 To cut them off, and from the earth
 blot out their hated name.
17 Deliv'rance to his ſaints he gives,
 when his relief they crave;
18 He's nigh to heal the broken heart,
 and contrite ſpirit ſave.
19 The wicked oft, but ſtill in vain,
 againſt the juſt conſpire;
20 For under their affliction's weight
 he keeps their bones entire.
21 The wicked, from their wicked arts,
 their ruin ſhall derive;
 Whilſt righteous men, whom they deteſt,
 ſhall them and theirs ſurvive.
22 For God preſerves the ſouls of thoſe
 who on his truth depend;
 To them, and their poſterity,
 his bleſſings ſhall deſcend.

PSALM XXXV.

1 AGainſt all thoſe that ſtrive with me,
 O Lord, aſſert my right;

PSALM XXXV.

With such as war unjustly wage,
   do thou my battles fight.
2 Thy buckler take, and bind thy shield
   upon thy warlike arm;
Stand up, O God, in my defence,
   and keep me safe from harm.
3 Bring forth thy spear; and stop their course,
   that haste my blood to spill;
Say to my soul, "I am thy health,
   "and will preserve thee still."
4 Let them with shame be cover'd o'er,
   who my destruction sought;
And such as did my harm devise,
   be to confusion brought.
5 Then shall they fly, dispers'd like chaff
   before the driving wind;
God's vengeful minister of wrath
   shall follow close behind.
6 And when, through dark and slipp'ry ways,
   they strive his rage to shun,
His vengeful ministers of wrath
   shall goad them as they run.
7 Since, unprovok'd by any wrong,
   they hid their treach'rous snare;
And, for my harmless soul, a pit
   did, without cause, prepare;
8 Surpris'd by mischiefs unforeseen,
   by their own arts betray'd,
Their feet shall fall into the net,
   which they for me had laid;
9 Whilst my glad soul shall God's great Name
   for this deliv'rance bless,
And, by his saving health secur'd,
   its grateful joy express.
10 My very bones shall say, "O Lord,
   "who can compare with thee?
"Who sett'st the poor and helpless man
   "from strong oppressors free."

PART II.

11 False witnesses, with forg'd complaints,
   against my truth combin'd;
And to my charge such things they laid,
   as I had ne'er design'd.
12 The good which I to them had done,
   with evil they repaid;
And did, by malice undeserv'd,
   My harmless life invade.

13 But as for me, when they were sick,
   I still in sackcloth mourn'd;
 I pray'd and fasted, and my pray'r
   to my own breast return'd.
14 Had they my friends or brethren been,
   I could have done no more;
 Nor with more decent signs of grief
   a mother's loss deplore.
15 How diff'rent did their carriage prove,
   in times of my distress!
 When they, in crowds together met,
   did savage joy express.
 The rabble too, in num'rous throngs,
   by their example came;
 And ceas'd not, with reviling words,
   to wound my spotless fame.
16 Scoffers, that noble tables haunt,
   and earn their bread with lies,
 Did gnash their teeth, and sland'ring jests
   maliciously devise.
17 But, Lord, how long wilt thou look on?
   on my behalf appear;
 And save my guiltless soul, which they,
   like rav'ning beasts would tear.

PART III.

18 So I, before the list'ning world,
   shall grateful thanks express;
 And where the great assembly meets,
   thy Name with praises bless.
19 Lord, suffer not my causeless foes,
   who me unjustly hate;
 With open joy, or secret signs,
   to mock my sad estate.
20 For they, with hearts averse to peace,
   industriously devise,
 Against the men of quiet minds
   to forge malicious lies.
21 Nor with these private arts content,
   aloud they vent their spite;
 And say, "At last we found him out,
  "he did it in our sight."
22 But thou, who dost both them and me
   with righteous eyes survey,
 Assert my innocence, O Lord,
   and keep not far away.
23 Stir up thyself in my behalf;
   to judgment, Lord, awake;
 Thy righteous servant's cause, O God,
   to thy decision take.

PSALM XXXVI.

24 Lord, as my heart has upright been,
    let me thy juſtice find;
Nor let my cruel foes obtain
    the triumph they defign'd.

25 O! let them not, amongſt themſelves,
    in boaſting language fay,
" At length our wiſhes are complete;
" at laſt he's made our prey."

26 Let ſuch as in my harm rejoic'd,
    for ſhame their faces hide;
And foul diſhonour wait on thoſe,
    that proudly me defy'd:

27 Whilſt they with chearful voices ſhout,
    who my juſt cauſe befriend;
And bleſs the Lord, who loves to make
    ſucceſs his ſaints attend.

28 So ſhall my tongue thy judgments ſing,
    inſpir'd with grateful joy;
And chearful hymns, in praiſe of thee,
    ſhall all my days employ.

PSALM XXXVI.

1 MY crafty foe, with flatt'ring art,
    his wicked purpoſe would difguiſe;
But reaſon whiſpers to my heart,
    he ne'er ſets God before his eyes.

2 He ſoothes himſelf, retir'd from ſight;
    ſecure he thinks his treach'rous game;
Till his dark plots, expos'd to light,
    their falſe contriver brand with ſhame.

3 In deeds he is my foe confeſs'd,
    whilſt with his tongue he ſpeaks me fair;
True wiſdom's baniſh'd from his breaſt,
    and vice has ſole dominion there.

4 His wakeful malice ſpends the night
    in forging his accurs'd deſigns;
His obſtinate, ungen'rous ſpite
    no execrable means declines.

5 But, Lord, thy mercy, my ſure hope,
    above the heav'nly orb aſcends;
Thy ſacred truth's unmeaſur'd ſcope
    beyond the ſpreading ſky extends.

6 Thy juſtice like the hills remains;
    unfathom'd depths thy judgments are;
Thy providence the world ſuſtains;
    the whole creation is thy care.

7 Since of thy goodneſs all partake,
    with what aſſurance ſhould the juſt

Thy shelt'ring wings their refuge make,
  and saints to thy protection trust!
8 Such guests shall to thy courts be led,
  to banquet on thy love's repast;
And drink, as from a fountain's head,
  of joys that shall for ever last.
9 With thee the springs of life remain;
  thy presence is eternal day:
10 O let thy saints thy favour gain;
  to upright hearts thy truth display.
11 Whilst pride's insulting foot would spurn,
  and wicked hands my life surprise,
12 Their mischiefs on themselves return;
  down, down they're fall'n, no more to rise.

PSALM XXXVII.

1 THough wicked men grow rich or great,
    Yet let not their successful state
  thy anger or thy envy raise;
2 For they, cut down like tender grass,
Or like young flow'rs, away shall pass,
  whose blooming beauty soon decays.
3 Depend on God, and him obey,
So thou within the land shalt stay,
  secure from danger and from want:
4 Make his commands thy chief delight;
And he, thy duty to requite,
  shall all thy earnest wishes grant.
5 In all thy ways trust thou the Lord,
And he will needful help afford,
  to perfect ev'ry just design;
6 He'll make, like light, serene and clear,
Thy clouded innocence appear,
  and as a mid-day sun to shine.
7 With quiet mind on God depend,
And patiently for him attend;
  nor let thy anger fondly rise,
Though wicked men with wealth abound,
And with success the plots are crown'd
  which they maliciously devise.
8 From anger cease, and wrath forsake;
Let no ungovern'd passion make
  thy wav'ring heart espouse their crime;
9 For God shall sinful men destroy;
Whilst only they the land enjoy,
  who trust on him, and wait his time.
10 How soon shall wicked men decay!
Their place shall vanish quite away,
  nor by the strictest search be found;

PSALM XXXVII.

11 Whilſt humble ſouls poſſeſs the earth,
Rejoicing ſtill with godly mirth,
   with peace and plenty always crown'd.

PART II.

12 While ſinful crowds, with falſe deſign,
Againſt the righteous few combine,
   and gnaſh their teeth and threat'ning ſtand;
13 God ſhall their empty plots deride,
And laugh at their defeated pride:
   he ſees their ruin near at hand.
14 They draw the ſword, and bend the bow,
The poor and needy to o'erthrow,
   and men of upright lives to ſlay;
15 But their ſtrong bows ſhall ſoon be broke,
Their ſharpen'd weapon's mortal ſtroke
   through their own hearts ſhall force its way.
16 A little, with God's favour bleſs'd,
That's by one righteous man poſſeſs'd,
   the wealth of many bad excels;
17 For God ſupports the juſt man's cauſe;
But as for thoſe that break his laws,
   their unſucceſsful pow'r he quells.
18 His conſtant care the upright guides,
And over all their life preſides;
   their portion ſhall for ever laſt:
19 They, when diſtreſs o'erwhelms the earth,
Shall be unmov'd, and ev'n in dearth
   the happy fruits of plenty taſte.
20 Not ſo the wicked man, and thoſe
Who proudly dare God's will oppoſe;
   deſtruction is their hapleſs ſhare:
Like fat of lambs, their hopes, and they,
Shall in an inſtant melt away,
   and vaniſh into ſmoke and air.

PART III.

21 While ſinners, brought to ſad decay,
Still borrow on, and never pay,
   the juſt have will and pow'r to give,
22 For ſuch as God vouchſafes to bleſs,
Shall peaceably the earth poſſeſs;
   and thoſe he curſes ſhall not live.
23 The good man's way is God's delight:
He orders all the ſteps aright
   of him that moves by his command;
24 Though he ſometimes may be diſtreſs'd,
Yet ſhall he ne'er be quite oppreſs'd;
   for God upholds him with his hand.

25 From my firſt youth, till age prevail'd,
　I never ſaw the righteous fail'd,
　　or want o'ertake his num'rous race ;
26 Becauſe compaſſion fill'd his heart,
　And he did chearfully impart,
　　God made his offspring's wealth increaſe.
27 With caution ſhun each wicked deed,
　In virtue's ways with zeal proceed,
　　and ſo prolong your happy days ;
28 For God, who judgment loves, does ſtill
　Preſerve his ſaints ſecure from ill,
　　while ſoon the wicked race decays.
29, 30, 31 The upright ſhall poſſeſs the land ;
　His portion ſhall for ages ſtand ;
　　his mouth with wiſdom is ſupply'd :
　His tongue by rules of judgment moves ;
　His heart the law of God approves ;
　　therefore his footſteps never ſlide.

PART IV.

32 In wait the watchful ſinner lies
　In vain the righteous to ſurpriſe ;
　　in vain his ruin does decree :
33 God will not him defenceleſs leave,
　To his revenge expos'd, but ſave ;
　　and when he's ſentenc'd ſet him free.
34 Wait ſtill on God ; keep his command,
　And thou, exalted in the land,
　　thy bleſs'd poſſeſſion ne'er ſhalt quit :
　The wicked ſoon deſtroy'd ſhall be,
　And at his diſmal tragedy
　　thou ſhalt a ſafe ſpectator ſit.
35 The wicked I in pow'r have ſeen,
　And, like a bay-tree, freſh and green,
　　that ſpreads its pleaſant branches round :
36 But he was gone as ſwift as thought ;
　And, though in ev'ry place I ſought,
　　no ſign or track of him I found.
37 Obſerve the perfect man with care,
　And mark all ſuch as upright are ;
　　their rougheſt days in peace ſhall end :
38 While on the latter end of thoſe,
　Who dare God's ſacred will oppoſe,
　　a common ruin ſhall attend.
39 God to the juſt will aid afford ;
　Their only ſafeguard is the Lord ;
　　their ſtrength in time of need is he :
40 Becauſe on him they ſtill depend,
　The Lord will timely ſuccour ſend,
　　and from the wicked ſet them free.

PSALM XXXVIII.

1 THY chaft'ning wrath, O Lord, reftrain,
　　though I deferve it all ;
　.Nor let at once on me the ftorm
　　of thy difpleafure fall.
2 In ev'ry wretched part of me
　　thy arrows deep remain ;
　Thy heavy hand's afflicting weight
　　I can no more fuftain.
3 My flefh is one continued wound,
　　thy wrath fo fiercely glows ;
　Betwixt my punifhment and guilt
　　my bones have no repofe.
4 My fins, which to a deluge fwell,
　　my finking head o'erflow,
　And, for my feeble ftrength to bear,
　　too vaft a burden grow.
5 Stench and corruption fill my wounds ;
　　my folly's juft return ;
6 With trouble I am warp'd and bow'd,
　　and all day long I mourn.
7 A loath'd difeafe afflicts my loins,
　　infecting ev'ry part ;
8 With ficknefs worn, I groan and roar
　　through anguifh of my heart.

PART II.

9 But, Lord, before thy fearching eyes
　　all my defires appear ;
　And fure my groans have been too loud,
　　not to have reach'd thine ear.
10 My heart's opprefs'd, my ftrength decay'd,
　　my eyes depriv'd of light ;
11 Friends, lovers, kinfmen gaze aloof
　　on fuch a difmal fight.
12 Meanwhile, the foes that feek my life
　　their fnares to take me fet ;
　Vent flanders, and contrive all day
　　to forge fome new deceit :
13 But I, as if both deaf and dumb,
　　nor heard, nor once reply'd ;
14 Quite deaf and dumb, like one whofe tongue
　　with confcious guilt is ty'd.
15 For, Lord, to thee I do appeal,
　　my innocence to clear ;
　Affur'd that thou, the righteous God,
　　my injur'd caufe wilt hear.
16 " Hear me," faid I, " left my proud foes
　　" a fpiteful joy difplay ;

" Infulting,

PSALM XXXIX.

"Infulting, if they fee my foot
"but once to go aftray."
17 And, with continual grief opprefs'd,
to fink I now begin;
18 To thee, O Lord, I will confefs,
to thee bewail my fin.
19 But whilft I languifh, my proud foes
their ftrength and vigour boaft;
And they that hate me without caufe
are grown a dreadful hoft.
20 Ev'n they whom I oblig'd, return
my kindnefs with defpite;
And are my enemies, becaufe
I choofe the path that's right.
21 Forfake me not, O Lord my God,
nor far from me depart;
22 Make hafte to my relief, O thou,
who my falvation art.

PSALM XXXIX.

1 REfolv'd to watch o'er all my ways,
I kept my tongue in awe;
I curb'd my hafty words, when I
the wicked profp'rous faw.
2 Like one that's dumb, I filent ftood,
and did my tongue refrain
From good difcourfe; but that reftraint
increas'd my inward pain.
3 My heart did glow with working thoughts,
and no repofe could take;
Till ftrong reflection fann'd the fire,
and thus at length I fpake:
4 Lord, let me know my term of days,
how foon my life will end:
The num'rous train of ills difclofe,
which this frail ftate attend.
5 My life, thou know'ft, is but a fpan;
a cypher fums my years;
And ev'ry man, in beft eftate,
but vanity appears.
6 Man, like a fhadow, vainly walks,
with fruitlefs cares opprefs'd;
He heaps up wealth, but cannot tell
by whom 'twill be poffefs'd.
7 Why then fhould I on worthlefs toys,
with anxious cares attend?
On thee alone my ftedfaft hope
fhall ever, Lord, depend.

8, 9 Forgive

PSALM XL.

8, 9 Forgive my sins; nor let me scorn'd
by foolish sinners be;
For I was dumb, and murmur'd not,
because 'twas done by thee.
10 The dreadful burden of thy wrath
in mercy soon remove;
Lest my frail flesh too weak to bear
the heavy load should prove.
11 For when thou chast'nest man for sin,
thou mak'st his beauty fade,
(So vain a thing is he!) like cloth
by fretting moths decay'd.
12 Lord, hear my cry, accept my tears,
and listen to my pray'r,
Who sojourn like a stranger here,
as all my fathers were.
13 O! spare me yet a little time;
my wasted strength restore,
Before I vanish quite from hence,
and shall be seen no more.

PSALM XL.

1 I Waited meekly for the Lord,
   till he vouchsaf'd a kind reply;
Who did his gracious ear afford,
and heard from heav'n my humble cry.
2 He took me from the dismal pit,
when founder'd deep in miry clay;
On solid ground he plac'd my feet,
and suffer'd not my steps to stray.
3 The wonders he for me has wrought
shall fill my mouth with songs of praise;
And others, to his worship brought,
to hopes of like deliv'rance raise.
4 For blessings shall that man reward,
who on th' Almighty Lord relies;
Who treats the proud with disregard,
and hates the hypocrite's disguise.
5 Who can the wond'rous works recount
which thou, O God, for us hast wrought?
The treasures of thy love surmount
the pow'r of numbers, speech, and thought.
6 I've learnt that thou hast not desir'd
off'rings and sacrifice alone;
Nor blood of guiltless beasts requir'd
for man's transgression to atone.
7 I therefore come—come to fulfil
the oracles thy books impart;
8 'Tis my delight to do thy will;
thy law is written in my heart.

PSALM XLI.
PART II.

9 In full assemblies I have told
   thy truth and righteousness at large;
Nor did, thou know'st, my lips withhold
   from utt'ring what thou gav'st in charge:
10 Nor kept within my breast confin'd
   thy faithfulness and saving grace;
But preach'd thy love, for all design'd,
   that all might that, and truth, embrace.
11 Then let those mercies I declar'd
   to others, Lord, extend to me;
Thy loving-kindness my reward,
   thy truth my safe protection be.
12 For I with troubles am distress'd,
   too numberless for me to bear;
Nor less with loads of guilt oppress'd,
   that plunge and sink me to despair.
As soon, alas! may I recount
   the hairs of this afflicted head;
My vanquish'd courage they surmount,
   and fill my drooping soul with dread.

PART III.

13 But, Lord, to my relief draw near,
   for never was more pressing need;
In my deliv'rance, Lord, appear,
   and add to that deliv'rance speed.
14 Confusion on their heads return,
   who to destroy my soul combine;
Let them, defeated, blush and mourn,
   ensnar'd in their own vile design.
15 Their doom let desolation be,
   with shame their malice be repaid,
Who mock'd my confidence in thee,
   and sport of my affliction made.
16 While those who humbly seek thy face,
   to joyful triumphs shall be rais'd;
And all who prize thy saving grace,
   with me resound, The Lord be prais'd.
17 Thus, wretched though I am and poor,
   of me th' Almighty Lord takes care:
Thou God, who only can'st restore,
   to my relief with speed repair.

PSALM XLI.

1 HAppy the man whose tender care
   relieves the poor distress'd!
When troubles compass him around,
   the Lord shall give him rest.
2 The Lord his life, with blessings crown'd,
   in safety shall prolong;

And

And disappoint the will of those
  that seek to do him wrong.
3 If he in languishing estate,
    oppress'd with sickness lie;
  The Lord will easy make his bed,
    and inward strength supply.
4 Secure of this, to thee, my God,
    I thus my pray'r address'd;
  " Lord, for thy mercy, heal my soul,
  " though I have much transgress'd."
5 My cruel foes, with sland'rous words,
    attempt to wound my fame;
  " When shall he die," say they, " and men
  " forget his very name?"
6 Suppose they formal visits make,
    'tis all but empty show;
  They gather mischief in their hearts,
    and vent it where they go.
7, 8 With private whispers, such as these,
    to hurt me they devise;
  " A sore disease afflicts him now;
  " he's fall'n no more to rise."
9 My own familiar bosom-friend,
    on whom I most rely'd,
  Has me, whose daily guest he was,
    with open scorn defy'd.
10 But thou my sad and wretched state,
    in mercy, Lord, regard;
  And raise me up, that all their crimes
    may meet their just reward.
11 By this I know thy gracious ear
    is open, when I call;
  Because thou suffer'st not my foes
    to triumph in my fall.
12 Thy tender care secures my life
    from danger and disgrace;
  And thou vouchsaf'st to set me still
    before thy glorious face.
13 Let therefore Israel's Lord and God
    from age to age be bless'd;
  And all the people's glad applause
    with loud Amens express'd.

PSALM XLII.

1 AS pants the hart for cooling streams,
    when heated in the chace;
  So longs my soul, O God, for thee,
    and thy refreshing grace.

PSALM XLIII.

2 For thee, my God, the living God,
   my thirsty soul doth pine;
O! when shall I behold thy face,
   thou Majesty Divine?

3 Tears are my constant food, while thus
   insulting foes upbraid;
" Deluded wretch! where's now thy God?
" and where his promis'd aid?"

4 I sigh, whene'er my musing thoughts
   those happy days present,
When I, with troops of pious friends,
   thy temple did frequent.
When I advanc'd with songs of praise,
   my solemn vows to pay,
And led the joyful sacred throng,
   that kept the festal day.

5 Why restless, why cast down, my soul?
   trust God; who will employ
His aid for thee, and change these sighs
   to thankful hymns of joy.

6 My soul's cast down, O God! but thinks
   on thee and Sion still;
From Jordan's bank, from Hermon's heights,
   and Mizar's humbler hill.

7 One trouble calls another on,
   and, gath'ring o'er my head,
Fall spouting down, till round my soul
   a roaring sea is spread.

8 But when thy presence, Lord of life,
   has once dispell'd this storm,
To thee I'll midnight anthems sing,
   and all my vows perform.

9 God of my strength, how long shall I,
   like one forgotten, mourn;
Forlorn, forsaken, and expos'd
   to my oppressor's scorn?

10 My heart is pierc'd, as with a sword,
   while thus my foes upbraid:
" Vain boaster, where is now thy God?
" and where his promis'd aid?"

11 Why restless, why cast down, my soul?
   hope still; and thou shalt sing
The praise of him who is thy God,
   thy health's eternal spring.

PSALM XLIII.

1 JUST Judge of heav'n, against my foes
   do thou assert my injur'd right;
O set me free, my God, from those
   that in deceit and wrong delight.

2 Since thou art still my only stay,
    why leav'st thou me in deep distress?
Why go I mourning all the day,
    whilst me insulting foes oppress?
3 Let me with light and truth be blest;
    be these my guides, to lead the way,
Till on thy holy hill I rest,
    and in thy sacred temple pray.
4 Then will I there fresh altars raise
    to God, who is my only joy;
And well-tun'd harps, with songs of praise,
    shall all my grateful hours employ.
5 Why then cast down, my soul? and why
    so much oppress'd with anxious care?
On God, thy God, for aid rely,
    who will thy ruin'd state repair.

PSALM XLIV.

1 O Lord, our fathers oft have told
    in our attentive ears,
Thy wonders, in their days perform'd,
    and elder times than theirs:
2 How thou, to plant them here, didst drive
    the heathen from this land,
Dispeopled by repeated strokes
    of thy avenging hand.
3 For not their courage, nor their sword,
    to them possession gave;
Nor strength, that from unequal force
    their fainting troops could save:
But thy right-hand, and pow'rful arm,
    whose succour they implor'd;
Thy presence with the chosen race,
    who thy great name ador'd.
4 As thee their God our fathers own'd,
    thou art our sov'reign King;
O! therefore, as thou did'st to them,
    to us deliv'rance bring.
5 Through thy victorious Name, our arms
    the proudest foes shall quell;
And crush them with repeated strokes,
    as oft as they rebel.
6 I'll neither trust my bow nor sword,
    when I in fight engage;
7 But thee, who hast our foes subdu'd,
    and sham'd their spiteful rage.
8 To thee the triumph we ascribe,
    from whom the conquest came:
In God, we will rejoice all day,
    and ever bless his Name.

PART II.

9 But thou haſt caſt us off; and now
   moſt ſhamefully we yield;
 For thou no more vouchſaf'ſt to lead
   our armies to the field:
10 Since when, to ev'ry upſtart foe
   we turn our backs in fight;
 And with our ſpoil their malice feaſt,
   who bear us antient ſpite.
11 To ſlaughter doom'd, we fall, like ſheep,
   into their butch'ring hands;
 Or (what's more wretched yet) ſurvive,
   diſpers'd through heathen lands.
12 Thy people thou haſt ſold for ſlaves,
   and ſet their price ſo low,
 That not thy treaſure, by the ſale,
   but their diſgrace, may grow.
13, 14 Reproach'd by all the nations round,
   the heathens by-word grown;
 Whoſe ſcorn of us is both in ſpeech,
   and mocking geſtures, ſhown.
15 Confuſion ſtrikes me blind; my face
   in conſcious ſhame I hide;
16 While we are ſcoff'd, and God blaſphem'd,
   by their licentious pride.

PART III.

17 On us this heap of woes is fall'n;
   all this we have endur'd;
 Yet have not, Lord, renounc'd thy Name,
   or faith to thee abjur'd:
18 But in thy righteous paths have kept
   our hearts and ſteps with care;
19 Though thou haſt broken all our ſtrength,
   and we almoſt deſpair.
20 Could we, forgetting thy great Name,
   on other gods rely,
21 And not the Searcher of all hearts
   the treach'rous crime deſcry?
22 Thou ſee'ſt what ſuff'rings, for thy ſake,
   we ev'ry day ſuſtain;
 All ſlaughter'd, or reſerv'd like ſheep
   appointed to be ſlain.
23 Awake, ariſe; let ſeeming ſleep
   no longer thee detain;
 Nor let us, Lord, who ſue to thee,
   for ever ſue in vain.
24 Oh! wherefore hideſt thou thy face
   from our afflicted ſtate,

25 Whose souls and bodies sink to earth
   with grief's oppressive weight.
26 Arise, O Lord, and timely haste
   to our deliv'rance make;
   Redeem us, Lord;—if not for ours,
   yet for thy mercy's sake.

PSALM XLV.

1 WHILE I the King's loud praise rehearse,
       indited by my heart,
   My tongue is like the pen of him
       that writes with ready art.
2 How matchless is thy form, O King!
       thy mouth with grace o'erflows;
   Because fresh blessings God on thee
       eternally bestows.
3 Gird on thy sword, most mighty Prince;
       and clad in rich array,
   With glorious ornaments of pow'r,
       majestic pomp display.
4 Ride on in state, and still protect
       the meek, the just, and true;
   Whilst thy right-hand, with swift revenge,
       does all thy foes pursue.
5 How sharp thy weapons are to them
       that dare thy pow'r despise!
   Down, down they fall, while through their heart
       the feather'd arrow flies.
6 But thy firm throne, O God, is fix'd,
       for ever to endure;
   Thy sceptre's sway shall always last,
       by righteous laws secure.
7 Because thy heart, by justice led,
       did upright ways approve,
   And hated still the crooked paths,
       where wand'ring sinners rove;
   Therefore did God, thy God, on thee
       the oil of gladness shed;
   And has, above thy fellows round,
       advanc'd thy lofty head.
8 With cassia, aloes, and myrrh,
       thy royal robes abound;
   Which, from the stately wardrobe brought,
       spread grateful odours round.
9 Among the honourable train
       did princely virgins wait;
   The queen was plac'd at thy right-hand,
       in golden robes of state.

PSALM XLVI.

PART II.

10 But thou, O royal bride, give ear,
and to my words attend;
Forget thy native country now,
and ev'ry former friend.
11 So shall thy beauty charm the King,
nor shall his love decay;
For he is now become thy Lord;
to him due rev'rence pay.
12 The Tyrian matrons, rich and proud,
shall humble presents make;
And all the wealthy nations sue
thy favour to partake.
13 The King's fair Daughter's fairer soul
all inward graces fill;
Her raiment is of purest gold,
adorn'd with costly skill.
14 She in her nuptial garments dress'd,
with needles richly wrought,
Attended by her virgin train,
shall to the King be brought.
15 With all the state of solemn joy
the triumph moves along;
Till, with wide gates, the royal court
receives the pompous throng.
16 Thou, in thy royal Father's room,
must princely sons expect;
Whom thou to diff'rent realms may'st send,
to govern and protect;
17 Whilst this my song to future times
transmits thy glorious name;
And makes the world, with one consent,
thy lasting praise proclaim.

PSALM XLVI.

1 GOD is our refuge in distress;
A present help when dangers press;
in him, undaunted, we'll confide;
2, 3 Though earth were from her centre tost,
And mountains in the ocean lost,
torn piece-meal by the roaring tide.
4 A gentler stream with gladness still .
The city of our Lord shall fill,
the royal seat of God most high:
5 God dwells in Sion, whose fair tow'rs
Shall mock th' assaults of earthly pow'rs,
while his Almighty aid is nigh.
6 In tumults when the heathen rag'd,
And kingdoms war against us wag'd,
he thunder'd, and dispers'd their pow'rs:

7 The

PSALM XLVIII.

7 The Lord of Hosts conducts our arms,
  Our tow'r of refuge in alarms,
    our fathers' Guardian-God, and ours.
8 Come, see the wonders he hath wrought,
  On earth what desolation brought;
    how he has calm'd the jarring world:
9 He broke the warlike spear and bow;
  With them their thund'ring chariots too
    into devouring flames were hurl'd.
10 Submit to God's Almighty sway;
  For him the heathen shall obey,
    and earth her Sov'reign Lord confess:
11 The God of Hosts conducts our arms,
  Our tow'r of refuge in alarms,
    as to our fathers in distress.

PSALM XLVII.

1, 2 O All ye people, clap your hands,
       and with triumphant voices sing;
  No force the mighty pow'r withstands
    of God, the universal King.
3, 4 He shall opposing nations quell,
    and with success our battles fight;
  Shall fix the place where we must dwell,
    the pride of Jacob, his delight.
5, 6 God is gone up, our Lord and King,
    with shouts of joy, and trumpets' sound,
  To him repeated praises sing,
    and let the chearful song rebound.
7, 8 Your utmost skill in praise be shown,
    for him, who all the world commands,
  Who sits upon his righteous throne,
    and spreads his sway o'er heathen lands.
9 Our chiefs and tribes, that far from hence
    to serve the God of Abr'am came,
  Found him their constant sure defence:
    how great and glorious is his Name!

PSALM XLVIII.

1 THE Lord, the only God, is great,
      and greatly to be prais'd
  In Sion, on whose happy mount
    his sacred throne is rais'd.
2 Her tow'rs, the joy of all the earth,
    with beauteous prospect rise;
  On her north side th' Almighty King's
    imperial city lies.
3 God in her palaces is known;
    his presence is her guard:

4 Confed'rate

4 Confed'rate kings withdrew their siege,
  and of success despair'd.
5 They view'd her walls, admir'd, and fled,
  with grief and terror struck;
6 Like women, whom the sudden pangs
  of travail had o'ertook.
7 No wretched crew of mariners
  appear like them forlorn,
  When fleets from Tarshish' wealthy coasts
  by eastern winds are torn.
8 In Sion we have seen perform'd
  a work that was foretold,
  In pledge that God, for times to come,
  his city will uphold.
9 Not in our fortresses and walls
  did we, O God, confide;
  But on the temple fix'd our hopes,
  in which thou dost reside.
10 According to thy sov'reign Name,
  thy praise through earth extends;
  Thy pow'rful arm, as justice guides,
  chastises or defends.
11 Let Sion's mount with joy resound;
  her daughters all be taught
  In songs his judgments to extol,
  who this deliv'rance wrought.
12 Compass her walls in solemn pomp;
  your eyes quite round her cast;
  Count all her tow'rs, and see if there
  you find one stone displac'd.
13 Her forts and palaces survey;
  observe their order well;
  That, with assurance, to your heirs,
  his wonders you may tell.
14 This God is ours, and will be ours,
  whilst we in him confide;
  Who, as he has preserv'd us now,
  till death will be our guide.

PSALM XLIX.

1, 2 LET all the list'ning world attend,
  and my instruction hear;
  Let high and low, and rich and poor,
  with joint consent give ear.
3 My mouth with sacred wisdom fill'd,
  shall good advice impart;
  The sound result of prudent thoughts,
  digested in my heart.

PSALM XLIX.

4 To parables of weighty sense
   I will my ear incline;
Whilst to my tuneful harp I sing
   dark words of deep design.
5 Why should my courage fail in times
   of danger and of doubt,
When sinners, that would me supplant,
   have compass'd me about?
6 Those men, that all their hope and trust
   in heaps of treasure place,
And boast in triumph, when they see
   their ill-got wealth increase,
7 Are yet unable from the grave
   their dearest friend to free;
Nor can, by force of bribes, reverse
   th' Almighty Lord's decree.
8, 9 Their vain endeavours they must quit;
   the price is held too high;
No sums can purchase such a grant,
   that man should never die.
10 Not wisdom can the wise exempt,
   nor fools their folly save;
But both must perish, and in death
   their wealth to others leave.
11 For though they think their stately seats
   shall ne'er to ruin fall,
But their remembrance last in lands
   which by their names they call;
12 Yet shall their fame be soon forgot,
   how great soe'er their state;
With beasts their memory, and they,
   shall share one common fate.

PART II.

13 How great their folly is, who thus
   absurd conclusions make!
And yet their children, unreclaim'd,
   repeat the gross mistake.
14 They all, like sheep to slaughter led,
   the prey of death are made;
Their beauty, while the just rejoice,
   within the grave shall fade.
15 But God will yet redeem my soul;
   and from the greedy grave
His greater pow'r shall set me free,
   and to himself receive.
16 Then fear not thou, when worldly men
   in envy'd wealth abound;
Nor though their prosp'rous house increase,
   with state and honour crown'd.

17 For when they're summon'd hence by death,
    they leave all this behind;
  No shadow of their former pomp
    within the grave they find:
18 And yet they thought their state was blest,
    caught in the flatt'rer's snare,
  Who with their vanity comply'd,
    and prais'd their worldly care.
19 In their forefathers steps they tread;
    and when, like them, they die,
  Their wretched ancestors and they
    in endless darkness lie.
20 For man, how great soe'er his state,
    unless he's truly wise,
  As like a sensual beast he lives,
    so like a beast he dies.

PSALM L.

1, 2 THE Lord hath spoke, the mighty God
       Hath sent his summons all abroad,
     from dawning light, till day declines:
   The list'ning earth his voice hath heard,
   And he from Sion hath appear'd,
     where beauty in perfection shines.

3, 4 Our God shall come, and keep no more
   Misconstru'd silence, as before;
     but wasting flames before him send:
   Around shall tempests fiercely rage,
   Whilst he does heav'n and earth engage
     his just tribunal to attend.

5, 6 Assemble all my saints to me,
   (Thus runs the great divine decree)
     that in my lasting cov'nant live,
   And off'rings bring with constant care:
   The heav'ns his justice shall declare;
     for God himself shall sentence give.

7, 8 Attend, my people; Israel, hear;
   Thy strong accuser I'll appear;
     thy God, thy only God, am I:
   'Tis not of off'rings I complain,
   Which, daily in my temple slain,
     my sacred altar did supply.

9 Will this alone atonement make?
    No bullock from thy stall I'll take,
      nor he-goat from thy fold accept:
10 The forest beasts, that range along,
     The cattle too, are all my own,
       that on a thousand hills are kept.

11 I know

PSALM LI.

11 I know the fowls, that build their nests
In craggy rocks; and savage beasts,
that loosely haunt the open fields:
12 If seiz'd with hunger I could be,
I need not seek relief from thee,
since the world's mine, and all it yields.
13 Think'st thou that I have any need
On slaughter'd bulls and goats to feed,
to eat their flesh and drink their blood?
14 The sacrifices I require,
Are hearts which love and zeal inspire,
and vows with strictest care made good.
15 In time of trouble call on me,
And I will set thee safe and free;
and thou returns of praise shalt make.
16 But to the wicked thus saith God:
How dar'st thou teach my laws abroad,
or in thy mouth my cov'nant take?
17 For stubborn thou, confirm'd in sin,
Hast proof against instruction been,
and of my word didst lightly speak:
18 When thou a subtle thief didst see,
Thou gladly with him didst agree,
and with adult'rers didst partake.
19 Vile slander is thy chief delight;
Thy tongue, by envy mov'd, and spite,
deceitful tales does hourly spread:
20 Thou dost with hateful scandals wound
Thy brother, and with lies confound
the offspring of thy mother's bed.
21 These things didst thou, whom still I strove
To gain with silence, and with love,
till thou didst wickedly surmise,
That I was such a one as thou;
But I'll reprove and shame thee now,
and set thy sins before thine eyes.
22 Mark this, ye wicked fools, lest I
Let all my bolts of vengeance fly,
whilst none shall dare your cause to own:
23 Who praises me, due honour gives;
And to the man that justly lives
my strong salvation shall be shown.

PSALM LI.

1 HAVE mercy, Lord, on me,
as thou wert ever kind;
Let me, opprefs'd with loads of guilt,
thy wonted mercy find.

2, 3 Wash

PSALM LI.

2, 3 Wash off my foul offence,
 and cleanse me from my sin;
For I confess my crime, and see
 how great my guilt has been.
4 Against thee, Lord, alone,
 and only in thy sight,
Have I transgress'd; and, though condemn'd,
 must own thy judgment right.
5 In guilt each part was form'd
 of all this sinful frame;
In guilt I was conceiv'd, and born
 the heir of sin and shame.
6 Yet thou, whose searching eye
 does inward truth require,
In secret didst with wisdom's laws
 my tender soul inspire.
7 With hyssop purge me, Lord,
 and so I clean shall be;
I shall with snow in whiteness vie,
 when purify'd by thee.
8 Make me to hear with joy
 thy kind forgiving voice;
That so the bones which thou hast broke
 may with fresh strength rejoice.
9, 10 Blot out my crying sins,
 nor me in anger view:
Create in me a heart that's clean,
 an upright mind renew.

PART II.

11 Withdraw not thou thy help,
 nor cast me from thy sight;
Nor let thy Holy Spirit take
 its everlasting flight.
12 The joy thy favour gives,
 let me again obtain;
And thy free Spirit's firm support
 my fainting soul sustain.
13 So I thy righteous ways
 to sinners will impart;
Whilst my advice shall wicked men
 to thy just laws convert.
14 My guilt of blood remove,
 my Saviour, and my God;
And my glad tongue shall loudly tell
 thy righteous acts abroad.
15 Do thou unlock my lips,
 with sorrow clos'd and shame;
So shall my mouth thy wond'rous praise
 to all the world proclaim.

16 Could

16 Could facrifice atone,
   whole flocks and herds fhould die;
   But on fuch off'rings thou difdain'ft
   to caft a gracious eye.
17 A broken fpirit is
   by God moft highly priz'd;
   By him a broken contrite heart
   fhall never be defpis'd.
18 Let Sion favour find,
   of thy good will affur'd;
   And thy own city flourifh long,
   by lofty walls fecur'd.
19 The juft fhall then attend,
   and pleafing tribute pay;
   And facrifice of choiceft kind
   upon thy altar lay.

PSALM LII.

1 IN vain, O man of lawlefs might,
   thou boaft'ft thyfelf in ill;
   Since God, the God in whom I truft,
   vouchfafes his favour ftill.
2 Thy wicked tongue doth fland'rous tales
   malicioufly devife;
   And, fharper than a razor fet,
   it wounds with treach'rous lies.
3, 4 Thy thoughts are more on ill than good,
   on lies than truth, employ'd;
   Thy tongue delights in words, by which
   the guiltlefs are deftroy'd.
5 God fhall for ever blaft thy hopes,
   and fnatch thee foon away;
   Nor in thy dwelling-place permit,
   nor in the world, to ftay.
6 The juft, with pious fear, fhall fee
   the downfall of thy pride;
   And at thy fudden ruin laugh,
   and thus thy fall deride:
7 " See there the man that haughty was,
   " who proudly God defy'd,
   " Who trufted in his wealth, and ftill
   " on wicked arts rely'd."
8 But I am like thofe olive-plants
   that fhade God's temple round;
   And hope with his indulgent grace
   to be for ever crown'd.
9 So fhall my foul, with praife, O God,
   extol thy wond'rous love;
   And on thy Name with patience wait;
   for this thy faints approve.

PSALM LIII.

1 THE wicked fools muſt ſure ſuppoſe
    that God is but a name;
This groſs miſtake their practice ſhows,
    ſince virtue all diſclaim.

2 The Lord look'd down from heav'ns high tow'r,
    the ſons of men to view;
To ſee if any own'd his pow'r,
    or truth or juſtice knew.

3 But all, he ſaw, were backward gone,
    degen'rate grown and baſe;
None for religion car'd, not one
    of all the ſinful race.

4 But are thoſe workers of deceit
    ſo dull and ſenſeleſs grown,
That they like bread my people eat,
    and God's juſt pow'r diſown?

5 Their cauſeleſs fear ſhall ſtrangely grow;
    and they, deſpis'd of God,
Shall ſoon be foil'd; his hand ſhall throw
    their ſhatter'd bones abroad.

6 Would he his ſaving pow'r employ
    to break our ſervile band,
Loud ſhouts of univerſal joy
    ſhould echo through the land.

PSALM LIV.

1, 2 LOrd, ſave me, for thy glorious name;
    and in thy ſtrength appear,
To judge my cauſe; accept my pray'r,
    and to my words give ear.

3 Mere ſtrangers, whom I never wrong'd,
    to ruin me deſign'd;
And cruel men, that fear no God,
    againſt my ſoul combin'd.

4, 5 But God takes part with all my friends,
    and he's the ſureſt guard;
The God of truth ſhall give my foes
    their falſhood's due reward;

6 While I my grateful off'rings bring,
    and ſacrifice with joy;
And in his praiſe my time to come
    delightfully employ.

7 From dreadful danger and diſtreſs
    the Lord hath ſet me free;
Through him ſhall I of all my foes
    the juſt deſtruction ſee.

PSALM LV.

1 GIVE ear, thou Judge of all the earth,
    and liften when I pray;
Nor from thy humble fuppliant turn
    thy glorious face away.
2 Attend to this my fad complaint,
    and hear my grievous moans;
While I my mournful cafe declare,
    with artlefs fighs and groans.
3 Hark how the foe infults aloud!
    how fierce oppreffors rage!
Whofe fland'rous tongues, with wrathful hate,
    againft my fame engage.
4, 5 My heart is rack'd with pain; my foul
    with deadly frights diftrefs'd;
With fear and trembling compafs'd round,
    with horror quite opprefs'd.
6 How often wifh'd I then, that I
    the dove's fwift wings could get;
That I might take my fpeedy flight,
    and feek a fafe retreat.
7, 8 Then would I wander far from hence,
    and in wild deferts ftray,
Till all this furious ftorm were fpent,
    this tempeft pafs'd away.

PART II.

9 Deftroy, O Lord, their ill defigns,
    their counfels foon divide;
For through the city my griev'd eyes
    have ftrife and rapine fpy'd.
10 By day and night, on ev'ry wall
    they walk their conftant round;
And in the midft of all her ftrength
    are grief and mifchief found.
11 Whoe'er through ev'ry part fhall roam,
    will frefh diforders meet;
Deceit and guile their conftant pofts
    maintain in ev'ry ftreet.
12 For 'twas not any open foe
    that falfe reflections made;
For then I could with eafe have borne
    the bitter things he faid;
'Twas none who hatred had profefs'd,
    that did againft me rife;
For then I had withdrawn myfelf
    from his malicious eyes.
13, 14 But 'twas e'en thou, my guide, my friend,
    whom tend'reft love did join;

Whose sweet advice I valued most;
whose pray'rs were mix'd with mine.
15 Sure vengeance, equal to their crimes,
such traitors must surprise,
And sudden death requite those ills
they wickedly devise.
16, 17 But I will call on God, who still
shall in my aid appear;
At morn, at noon, and night, I'll pray;
and he my voice shall hear.

PART III.

18 God has releas'd my soul from those
that did with me contend;
And made a 'num'rous host of friends
my righteous cause defend.
19 For he, who was my help of old,
shall now his suppliant hear;
And punish them whose prosp'rous state
makes them no God to fear.
20 Whom can I trust, if faithless men
perfidiously devise
To ruin me, their peaceful friend,
and break the strongest ties?
21 Though soft and melting are their words,
their hearts with war abound;
Their speeches are more smooth than oil,
and yet like swords they wound.
22 Do thou, my soul, on God depend,
and he shall thee sustain;
He aids the just, whom to supplant
the wicked strive in vain.
23 My foes, that trade in lies and blood,
shall all untimely die;
Whilst I, for health and length of days,
on thee, my God, rely.

PSALM LVI.

1 DO thou, O God, in mercy help;
for man my life pursues:
To crush me with repeated wrongs,
he daily strife renews.
2 Continually my spiteful foes
to ruin me combine;
Thou seest, who sitt'st enthron'd on high,
what mighty numbers join.
3 But though sometimes surpris'd by fear,
on danger's first alarm;
Yet still for succour I depend
on thy Almighty arm.

4 God's

4 God's faithful promise I shall praise,
   on which I now rely;
In God I trust, and, trusting him,
   the arm of flesh defy.
5 They wrest my words, and make them speak
   a sense they never meant;
Their thoughts are all, with restless spite,
   on my destruction bent.
6 In close assemblies they combine,
   and wicked projects lay;
They watch my steps, and lie in wait
   to make my soul their prey.
7 Shall such injustice still escape?
   O righteous God, arise;
Let thy just wrath, too long provok'd,
   this impious race chastise.
8 Thou numb'rest all my steps, since first
   I was compell'd to flee;
My very tears are treasur'd up,
   and register'd by thee.
9 When therefore I invoke thy aid,
   my foes shall be o'erthrown;
For I am well assur'd that God
   my righteous cause will own.
10, 11 I'll trust God's word, and so despise
   the force that man can raise;
12 To thee, O God, my vows are due;
   to thee I'll render praise.
13 Thou hast retriev'd my soul from death;
   and thou wilt still secure
The life thou hast so oft preserv'd,
   and make my footsteps sure:
14 That thus protected by thy pow'r,
   I may this light enjoy;
And in the service of my God
   my lengthen'd days employ.

PSALM LVII.

1 THY mercy, Lord, to me extend;
   On thy protection I depend;
And to thy wing for shelter haste,
Till this outrageous storm is pass'd.
2 To thy tribunal, Lord, I fly,
Thou sov'reign Judge, and God most high,
Who wonders hast for me begun,
And wilt not leave thy work undone.
3 From heaven protect me by thine arm,
And shame all those who seek my harm;
To my relief thy mercy send,
And truth, on which my hopes depend.

PSALM LVIII.

4 For I with savage men converse,
  Like hungry lions wild and fierce;
  With men whose teeth are spears, their words
  Invenom'd darts and two-edg'd swords.

5 Be thou, O God, exalted high;
  And, as thy glory fills the sky,
  So let it be on earth display'd,
  Till thou art here, as there, obey'd.

6 To take me they their net prepar'd,
  And had almost my soul ensnar'd;
  But fell themselves, by just decree,
  Into the pit they made for me.

7 O God, my heart is fix'd, 'tis bent,
  Its thankful tribute to present;
  And, with my heart, my voice I'll raise,
  To thee, my God, in songs of praise:

8 Awake, my glory; harp and lute,
  No longer let your strings be mute;
  And I, my tuneful part to take,
  Will with the early dawn awake.

9 Thy praises, Lord, I will resound
  To all the list'ning nations round;

10 Thy mercy highest heav'n transcends;
   Thy truth beyond the clouds extends.

11 Be thou, O God, exalted high;
   And, as thy glory fills the sky,
   So let it be on earth display'd,
   Till thou art here, as there, obey'd.

PSALM LVIII.

1 SPEAK, O ye judges of the earth,
    if just your sentence be;
  Or must not innocence appeal
    to heav'n from your decree?

2 Your wicked hearts and judgments are
    alike by malice sway'd;
  Your griping hands, by weighty bribes,
    to violence betray'd.

3 To virtue strangers, from the womb
    their infant steps went wrong;
  They prattled slander, and in lies
    employ'd their lisping tongue.

4 No serpent of parch'd Afric's breed
    does ranker poison bear;
  The drowsy adder will as soon
    unlock his sullen ear.

5 Unmov'd by good advice, and deaf
    as adders they remain;

From

PSALM LIX.

From whom the skilful charmer's voice
  can no attention gain.
6 Defeat, O God, their threat'ning rage,
  and timely break their pow'r;
Disarm these growling lions' jaws,
  e'er practis'd to devour.
7 Let now their insolence, at height,
  like ebbing tides be spent;
Their shiver'd darts deceive their aim,
  when they their bow have bent.
8 Like snails let them dissolve to slime;
  like hasty births, become
Unworthy to behold the sun,
  and dead within the womb.
9 E'er thorns can make the flesh-pots boil,
  tempestuous wrath shall come
From God, and snatch them hence alive
  to their eternal doom.
10 The righteous shall rejoice to see
  their crimes with vengeance meet;
And saints in persecutors' blood
  shall dip their harmless feet.
11 Transgressors then with grief shall see
  just men rewards obtain;
And own a God, whose justice will
  the guilty earth arraign.

PSALM LIX.

1 DEliver me, O Lord, my God,
  from all my spiteful foes;
In my defence oppose thy pow'r
  to theirs who me oppose.
2 Preserve me from a wicked race,
  who make a trade of ill;
Protect me from remorseless men,
  who seek my blood to spill.
3 They lie in wait, and mighty pow'rs
  against my life combine,
Implacable; yet, Lord, thou know'st,
  for no offence of mine.
4 In haste they run about, and watch
  my guiltless life to take;
Look down, O Lord, on my distress,
  and to my help awake.
5 Thou, Lord of Hosts, and Israel's God,
  their heathen rage suppress;
Relentless vengeance take on those
  who stubbornly transgress.

PSALM LIX.

6 At ev'ning, to befet my houfe,
   like growling dogs they meet;
   While others through the city range,
   and ranfack ev'ry ftreet.
7 Their throats envenom'd flander breathe;
   their tongues are fharpen'd fwords;
   " Who hears?" fay they, " or, hearing, dares
   " reprove our lawlefs words?"
8 But from thy throne thou fhalt, O Lord,
   their baffled plots deride;
   And foon to fhame and fcorn expofe
   their boafted heathen pride.
9 On thee I wait; 'tis on thy ftrength
   for fuccour I depend;
   'Tis thou, O God, art my defence,
   who only can defend.
10 Thy mercy, Lord, which has fo oft
   from danger fet me free,
   Shall crown my wifhes, and fubdue
   my haughty foes to me.
11 Deftroy them not, O Lord, at once;
   reftrain thy vengeful blow;
   Left we, ungratefully, too foon
   forget their overthrow.
   Difperfe them through the nations round
   by thy avenging pow'r;
   Do thou bring down their haughty pride,
   O Lord, our fhield and tow'r.
12 Now, in the height of all their hopes,
   their arrogance chaftife;
   Whofe tongues have finn'd without reftraint,
   and curfes join'd with lies.
13 Nor fhalt thou, whilft their race endures,
   thine anger, Lord, fupprefs;
   That diftant lands, by their juft doom,
   may Ifrael's God confefs.
14 At ev'ning let them ftill perfift
   like growling dogs to meet,
   Still wander all the city round,
   and traverfe ev'ry ftreet.
15 Then, as for malice now they do,
   for hunger let them ftray;
   And yell their vain complaints aloud,
   defeated of their prey.
16 Whilft early I thy mercy fing,
   thy wond'rous power confefs;
   For thou haft been my fure defence,
   my refuge in diftrefs.

17 To thee with never-ceasing praise,
   O God, my strength, I'll sing;
   Thou art my God, the Rock from whence
   my health and safety spring.

PSALM LX.

1 O God, who hast our troops disper'd,
   Forsaking those who left thee first;
   As we thy just displeasure mourn,
   To us, in mercy, Lord, return.
2 Our strength, that firm as earth did stand,
   Is rent by thy avenging hand;
   O! heal the breaches thou hast made:
   We shake, we fall, without thy aid!
3 Our folly's sad effects we feel;
   For, drunk with discord's cup we reel:
4 But now, for them who thee rever'd,
   Thou hast thy truth's bright banner rear'd.
5 Let thy right-hand thy saints protect;
   Lord, hear the pray'rs that we direct:
6 The holy God has spoke; and I,
   O'erjoy'd, on his firm word rely:
   To thee in portions I'll divide
   Fair Sichem's soil, Samaria's pride;
   To Sichem, Succoth next I'll join,
   And measure out her vale by line.
7 Manasseh, Gilead, both subscribe
   To my commands, with Ephraim's tribe;
   Ephraim by arms supports my cause,
   And Judah by religious laws.
8 Moab my slave and drudge shall be,
   Nor Eden from my yoke get free;
   Proud Palestine's imperious state
   Shall humbly on our triumph wait.
9 But who shall quell these mighty pow'rs,
   And clear my way to Edom's tow'rs?
   Or through her guarded frontiers tread
   The path that doth to conquest lead?
10 Ev'n thou, O God, who hast dispers'd
   Our troops (for we forsook thee first;)
   Those whom thou did'st in wrath forsake,
   Aton'd, thou wilt victorious make.
11 Do thou our fainting cause sustain;
   For human succours are but vain.
12 Fresh strength and courage God bestows:
   'Tis he treads down our proudest foes.

PSALM LXI.

1 LORD, hear my cry, regard my pray'r,
   which I, oppress'd with grief,

2 From earth's remoteft parts addrefs
   to thee for kind relief.
   O lodge me fafe beyond the reach
   of perfecuting pow'r;
3 Thou, who fo oft from fpiteful foes
   haft been my fhelt'ring tow'r.
4 So fhall I in thy facred courts
   fecure from danger lie;
   Beneath the covert of thy wings,
   all future ftorms defy.
5 In fign my vows are heard, once more
   I o'er my chofen reign;
6 O! blefs with long and profp'rous life
   the king thou didft ordain.
7 Confirm his throne, and make his reign
   accepted in thy fight;
   And let thy truth and mercy both
   in his defence unite.
8 So fhall I ever fing thy praife,
   thy Name for ever blefs;
   Devote my profp'rous days to pay
   the vows of my diftrefs.

PSALM LXII.

1, 2 MY foul for help on God relies;
        from him alone my fafety flows:
   My Rock, my Health, that ftrength fupplies
        to bear the fhock of all my foes.
3 How long will ye contrive my fall,
   which will but haften on your own?
   You'll totter like a bending wall,
   or fence of uncemented ftone.
4 To make my envy'd honours lefs
   they ftrive with lies, their chief delight;
   For they, tho' with their mouths they blefs,
   in private curfe with inward fpite.
5, 6 But thou, my foul, on God rely;
   on him alone thy truft repofe:
   My Rock and Health will ftrength fupply
   to bear the fhock of all my foes.
7 God does his faving health difpenfe,
   and flowing bleffings daily fend:
   He is my fortrefs and defence;
   on him my foul fhall ftill depend.
8 In him, ye people, always truft;
   before his throne pour out your hearts;
   For God, the merciful and juft,
   his timely aid to us imparts.

PSALM LXIII.

9 The vulgar fickle are and frail;
   the great diffemble and betray;
   And, laid in truth's impartial fcale,
   the lighteft things will both out-weigh.
10 Then truft not in oppreffive ways;
   by fpoil and rapine grow not vain;
   Nor let your hearts, if wealth increafe,
   be fet too much upon your gain.
11 For God has oft his will exprefs'd,
   and I this truth have fully known;
   To be of boundlefs pow'r poffefs'd,
   belongs, of right, to God alone.
12 Though mercy is his darling grace,
   in which he chiefly takes delight;
   Yet will he all the human race
   according to their works requite.

PSALM LXIII.

1 O God, my gracious God, to thee
   My morning pray'rs fhall offer'd be;
   for thee my thirfty foul does pant:
   My fainting flefh implores thy grace
   Within this dry and barren place,
   where I refrefhing waters want.
2 O! to my longing eyes, once more,
   That view of glorious pow'r reftore,
   which thy majeftic houfe difplays:
3 Becaufe to me thy wond'rous love
   Than life itfelf does dearer prove,
   my lips fhall always fpeak thy praife.
4 My life, while I that life enjoy,
   In bleffing God I will employ;
   with lifted hands adore his name:
5 My foul's content fhall be as great
   As theirs who choiceft dainties eat,
   while I with joy his praife proclaim.
6 When down I lie, fweet fleep to find,
   Thou, Lord, art prefent to my mind;
   and when I wake in dead of night:
7 Becaufe thou ftill doft fuccour bring,
   Beneath the fhadow of thy wing
   I reft with fafety and delight.
8 My foul, when foes would me devour,
   Cleaves faft to thee, whofe matchlefs pow'r,
   in her fupport is daily fhown:
9 But thofe the righteous Lord fhall flay,
   That my deftruction wifh; and they
   that feek my life, fhall lofe their own.

10 They by untimely ends shall die,
   Their flesh a prey to foxes lie;
     but God shall fill the king with joy:
11 Who thee confess shall still rejoice;
   Whilst the false tongue, and lying voice,
     thou, Lord, shalt silence and destroy.

PSALM LXIV.

1 LORD, hear the voice of my complaint
   to my request give ear;
Preserve my life from cruel foes,
   and free my soul from fear.
2 O! hide me with thy tend'rest care,
   in some secure retreat,
From sinners that against me rise,
   and all their plots defeat.
3 See how, intent to work my harm,
   they whet their tongues like swords;
And bend their bows to shoot their darts,
   sharp lies, and bitter words.
4 Lurking in private, at the just
   they take their secret aim;
And suddenly at him they shoot,
   quite void of fear and shame.
5 To carry on their ill designs
   they mutually agree;
They speak of laying private snares,
   and think that none shall see.
6 With utmost diligence and care
   their wicked plots they lay;
The deep designs of all their hearts
   are only to betray.
7 But God, to anger justly mov'd,
   his dreadful bow shall bend,
And on his flying arrow's point
   shall swift destruction send.
8 Those slanders which their mouths did vent,
   upon themselves shall fall;
Their crimes disclos'd shall make them be
   despis'd and shunn'd by all.
9 The world shall then God's pow'r confess,
   and nations trembling stand,
Convinc'd that 'tis the mighty work
   of his avenging hand:
10 Whilst righteous men, whom God secures,
   in him shall gladly trust;
And all the list'ning earth shall hear
   loud triumphs of the just.

PSALM LXV.

1 FOR thee, O God, our constant praise
  in Sion waits, thy chosen seat;
  Our promis'd altars there we'll raise,
  and all our zealous vows complete.
2 O thou, who to my humble pray'r
  didst always bend thy list'ning ear,
  To thee shall all mankind repair,
  and at thy gracious throne appear.
3 Our sins, though numberless, in vain
  to stop thy flowing mercy try;
  Whilst thou o'erlook'st the guilty stain,
  and washeth out the crimson dye.
4 Blest is the man who, near thee plac'd,
  within thy sacred dwelling lives!
  Whilst we at humble distance taste
  the vast delights thy temple gives.
5 By wond'rous acts, O God most just,
  have we thy gracious answer found:
  In thee remotest nations trust,
  and those whom stormy waves surround.
6, 7 God, by his strength, sets fast the hills,
  and does his matchless pow'r engage,
  With which the sea's loud waves he stills,
  and angry crowd's tumultuous rage.

PART II.

8 Thou, Lord, dost barb'rous lands dismay,
  when they thy dreadful tokens view;
  With joy they see the night and day
  each other's track, by turns, pursue.
9 From out thy unexhausted store
  thy rain relieves the thirsty ground;
  Makes lands, that barren were before,
  with corn and useful fruits abound.
10 On rising ridges down it pours,
  and ev'ry furrow'd valley fills;
  Thou mak'st them soft with gentle show'rs,
  in which a blest increase distils.
11 Thy goodness does the circling year
  with fresh returns of plenty crown;
  And where thy glorious paths appear,
  the fruitful clouds drop fatness down.
12 They drop on barren forests, chang'd
  by them to pastures fresh and green;
  The hills about, in order rang'd,
  in beauteous robes of joy are seen.
13 Large flocks with fleecy wool adorn
  the chearful downs; the vallies bring
  A plenteous crop of full-ear'd corn,
  and seem, for joy to shout and sing.

PSALM

PSALM LXVI.

1, 2 LET all the lands, with shouts of joy,
        to God their voices raise;
    Sing psalms in honour of his Name,
        and spread his glorious praise.
3 And let them say, How dreadful, Lord,
        in all thy works, art thou!
    To thy great pow'r thy stubborn foes
        shall all be forc'd to bow.
4 Through all the earth the nations round
        shall thee their God confess;
    And, with glad hymns, their awful dread
        of thy great Name express.
5 O! come, behold the works of God;
        and then with me you'll own,
    That he to all the sons of men
        has wond'rous judgment shown.
6 He made the sea become dry land,
        through which our fathers walk'd;
    Whilst to each other of his might
        with joy his people talk'd.
7 He, by his pow'r, for ever rules;
        his eyes the world survey:
    Let no presumptuous man rebel
        against his sov'reign sway.

PART II.

8, 9 O! all ye nations, bless our God,
        and loudly speak his praise;
    Who keeps our souls alive, and still
        confirms our stedfast ways.
10 For thou hast try'd us, Lord, as fire
        does try the precious ore;
11 Thou brought'st us into straits, where we
        oppressing burdens bore.
12 Insulting foes did us, their slaves,
        through fire and water chase;
    But yet, at last, thou brought'st us forth
        into a wealthy place.
13 Burnt off'rings to thy house I'll bring,
        and there my vows will pay,
14 Which I with solemn zeal did make
        in trouble's dismal day.
15 Then shall the richest incense smoke,
        the fattest rams shall fall,
    The choicest goats from out the fold,
        and bullocks from the stall.
16 O! come, all ye that fear the Lord,
        attend with heedful care,

Whilst

Whilst I what God for me has done
  with grateful joy declare.
17, 18 As I before his aid implor'd,
  so now I praise his Name;
Who, if my heart had harbour'd sin,
  would all my pray'rs disclaim.
19 But God to me, whene'er I cry'd,
  his gracious ear did bend,
And to the voice of my request
  with constant love attend.
20 Then bless'd for ever be my God,
  who never, when I pray,
Withholds his mercy from my soul,
  nor turns his face away.

PSALM LXVII.

1 TO bless thy chosen race,
    in mercy, Lord, incline;
  And cause the brightness of thy face
    on all thy saints to shine:
2 That so thy wond'rous way
    may through the world be known;
  While distant lands their tribute pay,
    and thy salvation own.
3 Let diff'ring nations join
    to celebrate thy fame;
  Let all the world, O Lord, combine
    to praise thy glorious Name.
4 O let them shout and sing
    with joy and pious mirth;
  For thou, the righteous Judge and King,
    shalt govern all the earth.
5 Let diff'ring nations join
    to celebrate thy fame;
  Let all the world, O Lord, combine
    to praise thy glorious Name.
6 Then shall the teeming ground
    a large increase disclose;
  And we with plenty shall be crown'd,
    which God, our God, bestows.
7 Then God upon our land
    shall constant blessings show'r;
  And all the world in awe shall stand
    of his resistless pow'r.

PSALM LXVIII.

1 LET God, the God of battle, rise,
    and scatter his presumptuous foes;
  Let shameful rout their host surprise,
    who spitefully his power oppose.

PSALM LXVIII.

2 As smoke in tempest's rage is lost,
    or wax into the furnace cast;
  So let their sacrilegious host
    before his wrathful presence waste.
3 But let the servants of his will
    his favour's gentle beams enjoy;
  Their upright hearts let gladness fill,
    and chearful songs their tongues employ.
4 To him your voice in anthem's raise;
    Jehovah's awful name he bears:
  In him rejoice, extol his praise,
    who rides upon high-rolling spheres.
5 Him, from his empire of the skies,
    to this low world compassion draws,
  The orphan's claim to patronize,
    and judge the injur'd widow's cause.
6 'Tis God, who from a foreign soil
    restores poor exiles to their home;
  Makes captives free, and fruitless toil
    their proud oppressors' righteous doom.
7 'Twas so of old, when thou didst lead
    in person, Lord, our armies forth;
  Strange terrors through the desert spread,
    convulsions shook th' astonish'd earth.
8 The breaking clouds did rain distil,
    and heav'n's high arches shook with fear:
  How then should Sinai's humble hill
    of Israel's God the presence bear?
9 Thy hand, at famish'd earth's complaint,
    reliev'd her from celestial stores,
  And when thy heritage was faint,
    assuag'd the drought with plenteous show'rs.
10 Where savages had rang'd before,
    at ease thou mad'st our tribes reside;
   And, in the desert, for the poor
    thy gen'rous bounty did provide.

PART II.

11 Thou gav'st the word; we sally'd forth,
    and in that pow'rful word o'ercame;
   While virgin-troops with songs of mirth,
    in state our conquest did proclaim.
12 Vast armies, by such gen'rals led,
    as yet had ne'er receiv'd a foil,
   Forsook their camp with sudden dread,
    and to our women left the spoil.
13 Though Egypt's drudges you have been,
    your army's wing shall shine as bright
   As doves, in golden sunshine seen,
    or silver'd o'er with paler light.

PSALM LXVIII.

14 'Twas so, when God's almighty hand
    o'er scatter'd kings the conquest won;
  Our troops, drawn up on Jordan's strand,
    high Salmon's glitt'ring snow outshone.
15 From thence to Jordan's farther coast,
    and Bashan's hill we did advance:
  No more her height shall Bashan boast,
    but that she's God's inheritance.
16 But wherefore (though the honour's great)
    should this, O mountain, swell your pride?
  For Sion is his chosen seat,
    where he for ever will reside.
17 His chariots numberless; his pow'rs
    are heav'nly hosts, that wait his will;
  His presence now fills Sion's tow'rs,
    as once it honour'd Sinai's hill.
18 Ascending high, in triumph thou
    captivity hast captive led;
  And on thy people did'st bestow
    the spoil of armies once their dread.
  E'en rebels shall partake thy grace,
    and humble proselytes repair
  To worship at thy dwelling-place,
    and all the world pay homage there.
19 For benefits each day bestow'd,
    be daily his great Name ador'd,
20 Who is our Saviour, and our God,
    of life and death the sov'reign Lord.
21 But justice for his harden'd foes
    proportion'd vengeance hath decreed,
  To wound the hoary head of those,
    who in presumptuous crimes proceed.
22 The Lord hath thus in thunder spoke:
  " As I subdu'd proud Bashan's king,
  " Once more I'll break my people's yoke,
  " and from the deep my servants bring.
23 " Their feet shall with a crimson flood
  " of slaughter'd foes be cover'd o'er;
  " Nor earth receive such impious blood,
  " but leave for dogs th' unhallow'd gore."

PART III.

24 When, marching to thy blest abode,
    the wond'ring multitude survey'd
  The pompous state of thee, our God,
    in robes of majesty array'd;
25 Sweet-singing Levites led the van;
    loud instruments brought up the rear;
  Between both troops, a virgin-train
    with voice and timbrel charm'd the ear.

26 This was the burden of their song:
  " In full assemblies bless the Lord;
  " All who to Israel's tribes belong,
   " of Israel's God the praise record."
27 Nor little Benjamin alone
    from neighb'ring bounds did there attend,
  Nor only Judah's nearer throne
    her counsellors in state did send;
  But Zebulon's remoter seat,
    and Napthali's more distant coast,
  The grand procession to complete,
    sent up their tribes, a princely host.
28 Thus God to strength and union brought
    our tribes, at strife till that blest hour,
  This work, which thou, O God, hast wrought,
    confirm with fresh recruits of pow'r.
29 To visit Salem, Lord, descend,
    and Sion, thy terrestrial throne;
  Where kings with presents shall attend,
    and thee with offer'd crowns atone.
30 Break down the spearmens' ranks, who threat
    like pamper'd herds of savage might;
  Their silver-armour'd chiefs defeat,
    who in destructive war delight.
31 Egypt shall then to God stretch forth
    her hands, and Afric homage bring;
32 The scatter'd kingdoms of the earth
    their common Sov'reign's praises sing;
33 Who, mounted on the loftiest sphere
    of ancient heav'n, sublimely rides;
  From whence his dreadful voice we hear,
    like that of warring winds and tides.
34 Ascribe the pow'r to God most high:
    of humble Israel he takes care;
  Whose strength, from out the dusky sky,
    darts shining terrors through the air.
35 How dreadful are the sacred courts,
    where God has fix'd his earthly throne!
  His strength his feeble saints supports,
    to give God praise, and him alone.

PSALM LXIX.

1 SAVE me, O God, from waves that roll,
    And press to overwhelm my soul:
2 With painful steps in mire I tread,
  And deluges o'erflow my head.
3 With restless cries my spirits faint,
  My voice is hoarse with long complaint;
  My sight decays with tedious pain,
  Whilst for my God I wait in vain.

4 My

PSALM LXIX.

4 My hairs, though num'rous, are but few
 Compar'd with foes that me pursue
 With groundless hate; grown now of might
 To execute their lawless spite,
 They force me, guiltless to resign,
 As rapine, what by right was mine:
5 Thou, Lord, my innocence doth see,
 Nor are my sins conceal'd from thee.
6 Lord God of hosts, take timely care,
 Lest, for my sake, thy saints despair;
7 Since I have suffer'd for thy Name
 Reproach, and hid my face in shame:
8 A stranger to my country grown,
 Nor to my nearest kindred known;
 A foreigner, expos'd to scorn
 By brethren of my mother born.
9 For zeal to thy lov'd house and Name
 Consumes me like devouring flame;
 Concern'd at their affronts to thee,
 More than at slanders cast on me.
10 My very tears and abstinence
 They construe in a spiteful sense:
11 When cloath'd with sackcloth for their sake,
 They me their common proverb make.
12 Their judges at my wrongs do jest,
 Those wrongs they ought to have redress'd:
 How should I then expect to be
 From libels of lewd drunkards free?
13 But, Lord, to thee I will repair
 For help, with humble, timely pray'r;
 Relieve me from thy mercy's store;
 Display thy truth's preserving pow'r.
14 From threat'ning dangers me relieve,
 And from the mire my feet retrieve;
 From spiteful foes in safety keep,
 And snatch me from the raging deep.
15 Controul the deluge, ere it spread,
 And roll its waves above my head;
 Nor deep destruction's open pit
 To close her jaws on me permit.
16 Lord, hear the humble pray'r I make,
 For thy transcending goodness' sake;
 Relieve thy supplicant once more
 From thy abounding mercy's store.
17 Nor from thy servant hide thy face;
 Make haste, for desp'rate is my case;
18 Thy timely succour interpose,
 And shield me from remorseless foes.

PSALM LXIX.

19 Thou know'ſt what infamy and ſcorn
   I from my enemies have borne;
   Nor can their cloſe diſſembled ſpite,
   Or darkeſt plots, eſcape thy ſight.
20 Reproach and grief have broke my heart;
   I look'd for ſome to take my part,
   To pity or relieve my pain;
   But look'd, alas! for both in vain.
21 With hunger pin'd, for food I call;
   Inſtead of food, they give me gall;
   And when with thirſt my ſpirits ſink,
   They give me vinegar to drink.
22 Their tables, therefore, to their health
   Shall prove a ſnare, a trap their wealth;
23 Perpetual darkneſs ſeize their eyes,
   And ſudden blaſts their hopes ſurpriſe.
24 On them thou ſhalt thy fury pour,
   Till thy fierce wrath their race devour;
25 And make their houſe a diſmal cell,
   Where none will e'er vouchſafe to dwell.
26 For new afflictions they procur'd
   For him who had thy ſtripes endur'd;
   And made the wound thy ſcourge had torn,
   To bleed afreſh, with ſharper ſcorn.
27 Sin ſhall to ſin their ſteps betray,
   Till they to truth have loſt the way:
28 From life thou ſhalt exclude their ſoul,
   Nor with the juſt their names enrol.
29 But me, howe'er diſtreſs'd and poor,
   Thy ſtrong ſalvation ſhall reſtore;
30 Thy pow'r with ſongs I'll then proclaim,
   And celebrate with thanks thy Name.
31 Our God ſhall this more highly prize,
   Than herds or flocks in ſacrifice;
32 Which humble ſaints with joy ſhall ſee,
   And hope for like redreſs with me.
33 For God regards the poor's complaint;
   Sets priſ'ners free from cloſe reſtraint:
34 Let heav'n, earth, ſea, their voices raiſe,
   And all the world reſound his praiſe.
35 For God will Sion's walls erect;
   Fair Judah's cities he'll protect;
   Till all her ſcatter'd ſons repair
   To undiſturb'd poſſeſſion there.
36 This bleſſing they ſhall, at their death,
   To their religious heirs bequeath;
   And they to endleſs ages more
   Of ſuch as his bleſt Name adore.

PSALM LXX.

1 O Lord, to my relief draw near;
　　for never was more preſſing need;
　For my deliv'rance, Lord, appear,
　　and add to that deliv'rance ſpeed.
2 Confuſion on their heads return
　　who to deſtroy my ſoul combine;
　Let them, defeated, bluſh and mourn,
　　enſnar'd in their own vile deſign.
3 Their doom let deſolation be;
　　with ſhame their malice be repaid,
　Who mock'd my confidence in thee,
　　and ſport of my afflictions made.
4 While thoſe who humbly ſeek thy face,
　　to joyful triumphs ſhall be rais'd;
　And all who prize thy ſaving grace,
　　with me ſhall ſing, The Lord be prais'd.
5 Thus, wretched though I am and poor,
　　the Mighty Lord of me takes care:
　Thou, God, who only can'ſt reſtore,
　　to my relief with ſpeed repair.

PSALM LXXI.

1, 2 IN thee I put my ſtedfaſt truſt;
　　defend me, Lord, from ſhame;
　Incline thine ear, and ſave my ſoul;
　　for righteous is thy Name.
3 Be thou my ſtrong abiding-place,
　　to which I may reſort;
　'Tis thy decree that keeps me ſafe;
　　thou art my rock and fort.
4, 5 From cruel and ungodly men
　　protect and ſet me free;
　For, from my earlieſt youth till now,
　　my hope has been in thee.
6 Thy conſtant care did ſafely guard
　　my tender infant days;
　Thou took'ſt me from my mother's womb,
　　to ſing thy conſtant praiſe.
7, 8 While ſome on me with wonder gaze,
　　thy hand ſupports me ſtill;
　Thy honour, therefore, and thy praiſe,
　　my mouth ſhall always fill.
9 Reject not then, thy ſervant, Lord,
　　when I with age decay;
　Forſake me not when, worn with years,
　　my vigour fades away.
10 My foes againſt my fame and me
　　with crafty malice ſpeak;

PSALM LXXI.

Againſt my ſoul they lay their ſnares,
    and mutual counſel take :
11 " His God," ſay they, " forſakes him now
    " on whom he did rely ;
    " Purſue and take him, whilſt no hope
    " of timely aid is nigh."
12 But thou, my God, withdraw not far,
    for ſpeedy help I call ;
13 To ſhame and ruin bring my foes,
    that ſeek to work my fall.
14 But as for me, my ſtedfaſt hope
    ſhall on thy pow'r depend ;
And I in grateful ſongs of praiſe
    my time to come will ſpend.

PART II.

15 Thy righteous acts, and ſaving health,
    my mouth ſhall ſtill declare ;
Unable yet to count them all,
    though ſumm'd with utmoſt care.
16 While God vouchſafes me his ſupport,
    I'll in his ſtrength go on ;
All other righteouſneſs diſclaim,
    and mention his alone.
17 Thou, Lord, haſt taught me from my youth
    to praiſe thy glorious Name ;
And, ever ſince, thy wond'rous works
    have been my conſtant theme.
18 Then now forſake me not, when I
    am grey and feeble grown ;
Till I to theſe and future times
    thy ſtrength and pow'r have ſhown.
19 How high thy juſtice ſoars, O God !
    how great and wond'rous are
The mighty works which thou haſt done !
    who may with thee compare !
20 Me, whom thy hand has ſorely preſs'd,
    thy grace ſhall yet relieve ;
And from the loweſt depth of woe,
    with tender care retrieve.
21 Through thee, my time to come ſhall be
    with pow'r and greatneſs crown'd ;
And me, who diſmal years have paſs'd,
    thy comforts ſhall ſurround.
22 Then I with pſaltery and harp,
    thy truth, O Lord, will praiſe ;
To thee, the God of Jacob's race,
    my voice in anthems raiſe.
23 Then joy ſhall fill my mouth, and ſongs
    employ my chearful voice ;

PSALM LXXII.

My grateful foul, by thee redeem'd,
 shall in thy strength rejoice.
24 My tongue thy just and righteous acts
 shall all the day proclaim;
Because thou did'st confound my foes,
 and brought'st them all to shame.

PSALM LXXII.

1 LORD, let thy just decrees the king
 in all his ways direct;
And let his son, throughout his reign,
 thy righteous laws respect.
2 So shall he still thy people judge
 with pure and upright mind;
Whilst all the helpless poor shall him
 their just protector find.
3 Then hills and mountains shall bring forth
 the happy fruits of peace;
Which all the land shall own to be
 the work of righteousness:
4 Whilst he the poor and needy race
 shall rule with gentle sway;
And from their humble necks shall take
 oppressive yokes away.
5 In ev'ry heart thy awful fear
 shall then be rooted fast,
As long as sun and moon endure,
 or time itself shall last.
6 He shall descend like rain, that cheers
 the meadow's second birth;
Or like warm show'rs whose gentle drops
 refresh the thirsty earth.
7 In his blest days the just and good
 shall be with favour crown'd;
The happy land shall ev'ry where
 with endless peace abound.
8 His uncontroul'd dominion shall
 from sea to sea extend;
Begin at proud Euphrates' streams,
 at nature's limits end.
9 To him the savage nations round
 shall bow their servile heads;
His vanquish'd foes shall lick the dust,
 where he his conquests spreads.
10 The king of Tarshish, and the isles,
 shall costly presents bring;
From spicy Sheba gifts shall come,
 and wealthy Saba's king.

11 To him shall ev'ry king on earth
his humble homage pay;
And diff'ring nations gladly join
to own his righteous sway.
12 For he shall set the needy free,
when they for succour cry;
Shall save the helpless and the poor,
and all their wants supply.

PART II.

13 His providence for needy souls
shall due supplies prepare;
And over their defenceless lives
shall watch with tender care.
14 He shall preserve and keep their souls
from fraud and rapine free;
And, in his sight, their guiltless blood
of mighty price shall be.
15 Therefore shall God his life and reign
to many years extend;
Whilst eastern princes tribute pay,
and golden presents send.
For him shall constant pray'rs be made,
through all his prosp'rous days;
His just dominion shall afford
a lasting theme of praise.
16 Of useful grain, through all the land,
great plenty shall appear;
A handful sown on mountains-top,
a mighty crop shall bear:
Its fruits, like cedars shook by winds,
a rattling noise shall yield;
The city too shall thrive, and vie
for plenty with the field.
17 The mem'ry of his glorious Name
through endless years shall run;
His spotless fame shall shine as bright
and lasting as the sun.
In him the nations of the world
shall be completely bless'd,
And his unbounded happiness
by ev'ry tongue confess'd.
18 Then bless'd be God, the mighty Lord,
the God whom Israel fears;
Who only wond'rous in his works,
beyond compare appears.
19 Let earth be with his glory fill'd;
for ever bless his Name;
Whilst to his praise the list'ning world
their glad assent proclaim.

PSALM LXXIII.

1 AT length, by certain proofs, 'is plain
that God will to his saints be kind;
That all whose hearts are pure and clean,
shall his protecting favour find.

2, 3 Till this sustaining truth I knew,
my stagg'ring feet had almost fail'd;
I griev'd the sinners' wealth to view,
and envy'd when the fools prevail'd.

4, 5 They to the grave in peace descend,
and, whilst they live, are hale and strong;
No plagues or troubles them offend,
which oft to other men belong.

6, 7 With pride, as with a chain, they're held,
and rapine seems their robe of state;
Their eyes stand out, with fatness swell'd;
they grow, beyond their wishes, great.

8, 9 With hearts corrupt, and lofty talk,
oppressive methods they defend;
Their tongue through all the earth does walk;
their blasphemies to heav'n ascend.

10 And yet admiring crowds are found,
who servile visits duly make;
Because with plenty they abound,
of which their flatt'ring slaves partake.

11 Their fond opinions these pursue,
till they with them profanely cry,
" How should the Lord our actions view?
" can he perceive, who dwells so high?"

12 Behold the wicked! these are they,
who openly their sins profess;
And yet their wealth's increas'd each day,
and all their actions meet success.

13, 14 " Then have I cleans'd my heart," said I,
" and wash'd my hands from guilt, in vain,
" If all the day oppress'd I lie,
" and ev'ry morning suffer pain."

15 Thus did I once to speak intend;
but, if such things I rashly say,
Thy children, Lord, I must offend,
and basely should their cause betray.

PART II.

16, 17 To fathom this my thoughts I bent,
but found the case too hard for me;
Till to the house of God I went;
then I their end did plainly see.

18 How high soe'er advanc'd, they all
on slipp'ry places loosely stand;

Thence into ruin headlong fall,
caſt down by thy avenging hand.
19, 20 How dreadful and how quick their fate!
deſpis'd by thee, when they're deſtroy'd;
As waking men with ſcorn do treat
the fancies that their dreams employ'd.
21, 22 Thus was my heart with grief oppreſt,
my reins were rack'd with reſtleſs pains;
So ſtupid was I like a beaſt,
who no reflecting thought retains.
23, 24 Yet ſtill thy preſence me ſupply'd,
and thy right-hand aſſiſtance gave;
Thou firſt ſhalt with thy counſel guide,
and then to glory me receive.
25 Whom then in heaven, but thee alone,
have I, whoſe favour I require?
Throughout the ſpacious earth there's none
that I beſides thee can deſire.
26 My trembling fleſh, and aching heart,
may often fail to ſuccour me;
But God ſhall inward ſtrength impart,
and my eternal portion be.
27 For they that far from thee remove,
ſhall into ſudden ruin fall;
If after other gods they rove,
thy vengeance ſhall deſtroy them all.
28 But as for me, 'tis good and juſt,
that I ſhould ſtill to God repair;
In him I always put my truſt,
and will his wond'rous works declare.

PSALM LXXIV.

1 WHY haſt thou caſt us off, O God?
wilt thou no more return?
O! why againſt thy choſen flock
does thy fierce anger burn?
2 Think on thy ancient purchaſe, Lord,
the land that is thy own,
By thee redeem'd; and Sion's mount,
where once thy glory ſhone.
3 O! come and view our ruin'd ſtate;
how long our troubles laſt;
See how the foe, with wicked rage,
has laid thy temple waſte.
4 Thy foes blaſpheme thy Name: where late
thy zealous ſervants pray'd,
The heathen there, with haughty pomp,
their banners have diſplay'd.

5, 6 Thoſe

PSALM LXXIV.

5, 6 Those curious carvings, which did once
 advance the artist's fame,
With ax and hammer they destroy,
 like works of vulgar frame.
7 Thy holy temple they have burn'd;
 and what escap'd the flame,
Has been profan'd, and quite defac'd,
 though sacred to thy Name.
8 Thy worship wholly to destroy
 maliciously they aim'd;
And all the sacred places burn'd,
 where we thy praise proclaim'd.
9 Yet of thy presence thou vouchsaf'st
 no tender signs to send;
We have no prophet now, that knows
 when this sad state shall end.

PART II.

10 But, Lord, how long wilt thou permit
 th' insulting foe to boast?
Shall all the honour of thy Name
 for evermore be lost?
11 Why hold'st thou back thy strong right-hand,
 and on thy patient breast,
When vengeance calls to stretch it forth,
 so calmly lett'st it rest?
12 Thou heretofore, with kingly pow'r,
 in our defence hast fought;
For us, throughout the wond'ring world,
 hast great salvation wrought.
13 'Twas thou, O God, that didst the sea
 by thy own strength divide;
Thou brak'st the wat'ry monsters' heads;
 the waves o'erwhelm'd their pride.
14 The greatest, fiercest of them all,
 that seem'd the deep to sway,
Was by thy pow'r destroy'd, and made
 to savage beasts a prey.
15 Thou clav'st the solid rock, and mad'st
 the waters largely flow;
Again, thou mad'st through parted streams
 thy wand'ring people go.
16 Thine is the chearful day, and thine
 the black return of night;
Thou hast prepar'd the glorious sun,
 and ev'ry feebler light.
17 By thee the borders of the earth
 in perfect order stand;
The summer's warmth, and winter's cold,
 attend on thy command.

PART

PART III.

18 Remember, Lord, how scornful foes
   have daily urg'd our shame;
   And how the foolish people have
   blasphem'd thy holy Name.
19 O! free thy mourning turtle-dove,
   by sinful crowds beset;
   Nor the assembly of thy poor
   for evermore forget.
20 Thy ancient cov'nant, Lord, regard,
   and make thy promise good;
   For now each corner of the land
   is fill'd with men of blood.
21 O! let not the oppress'd return
   with sorrow cloath'd, and shame;
   But let the helpless and the poor
   for ever praise thy Name.
22 Arise, O God, in our behalf;
   thy cause and ours maintain;
   Remember how insulting fools
   each day thy Name profane.
23 Make thou the boastings of thy foes
   for evermore to cease;
   Whose insolence, if unchastis'd,
   will more and more increase.

PSALM LXXV.

1 TO thee, O God, we render praise,
   to thee, with thanks repair;
   For, that thy Name to us is nigh,
   thy wond'rous works declare.
2 In Israel when my throne is fix'd,
   with me shall justice reign:
3 The land with discord shakes; but I
   the sinking frame sustain.
4 Deluded wretches I advis'd
   their errors to redress;
   And warn'd bold sinners, that they should
   their swelling pride suppress.
5 Bear not yourselves so high, as if
   no pow'r could yours restrain;
   Submit your stubborn necks, and learn
   to speak with less disdain:
6 For that promotion, which to gain
   your vain ambition strives,
   From neither east nor west, nor yet
   from southern climes arrives.
7 For God the great disposer is,
   and sov'reign Judge alone,

Who cafts the proud to earth, and lifts
the humble to a throne.
8 His hand holds forth a dreadful cup;
with purple wine 'tis crown'd;
The deadly mixture, which his wrath
deals out to nations round.
Of this his faints fometimes may tafte;
but wicked men fhall fqueeze
The bitter dregs, and be condemn'd
to drink the very lees.
9 His prophet, I, to all the world
this meffage will relate;
The juftice then of Jacob's God
my fong fhall celebrate.
10 The wicked's pride I will reduce,
their cruelty difarm;
Exalt the juft and feat him high
above the reach of harm.

PSALM LXXVI.

1 IN Judah the Almighty's known,
Almighty there by wonders fhown:
his name in Jacob does excel:
2 His fanctu'ry in Salem ftands;
The Majefty that heav'n commands,
in Sion condefcends to dwell.
3 He brake the bow and arrows there,
The fhield, and temper'd fword, and fpear;
there flain the mighty army lay:
4 Whence Sion's fame through earth is fpread,
Of greater glory, greater dread,
than hills where robbers lodge their prey.
5 Their valiant chiefs, who came for fpoil,
Themfelves met there a fhameful foil:
fecurely down to fleep they lay;
But wak'd no more, their ftouteft band
Ne'er lifted one refifting hand
'gainft his, that did their legions flay.
6 When Jacob's God began to frown,
Both horfe and charioteers, o'erthrown,
together flept in endlefs night:
7 When thou, whom earth and heav'n revere,
Doft once with wrathful look appear,
what mortal pow'r can ftand thy fight?
8 Pronounc'd from heav'n, earth heard its doom;
Grew hufh'd with fear, when thou didft come
9 the meek with juftice to reftore:

10 The wrath of man shall yield thee praise;
   Its last attempts but serve to raise
   the triumphs of Almighty pow'r.
11 Vow to the Lord, ye nations; bring
   Vow'd presents to th' eternal King:
   thus to his Name due rev'rence pay,
12 Who proudest potentates can quell,
   To earthly kings more terrible,
   than to their trembling subjects they.

PSALM LXXVII.

1 TO God I cry'd, who to my help
   did graciously repair:
2 In trouble's dismal day I sought
   my God with humble pray'r.
   All night my fest'ring wound did run;
   no med'cine gave relief:
   My soul no comfort would admit;
   my soul indulg'd her grief.
3 I thought on God, and favours past;
   but that increas'd my pain:
   I found my spirit more oppress'd,
   the more I did complain.
4 Through ev'ry watch of tedious night
   thou keep'st my eyes awake:
   My grief is swell'd to that excess,
   I sigh, but cannot speak.
5 I call'd to mind the days of old,
   with signal mercy crown'd;
   Those famous years of ancient times,
   for miracles renown'd.
6 By night I recollect my songs,
   on former triumphs made;
   Then search, consult, and ask my heart,
   where's now that wond'rous aid?
7 Has God for ever cast us off?
   withdrawn his favours quite?
8 Are both his mercy and his truth
   retir'd to endless night?
9 Can his long-practis'd love forget
   its wonted aids to bring?
   Has he in wrath shut up and seal'd
   his mercy's healing spring?
10 I said, my weakness hints these fears;
   but I'll my fears disband;
   I'll yet remember the Most High,
   and years of his right-hand.
11 I'll call to mind his works of old,
   the wonders of his might;

PSALM LXXVIII.

12 On them my heart shall meditate,
    my tongue shall them recite.
13 Safe lodg'd from human search on high,
    O God, thy counsels are!
  Who is so great a God as ours?
    who can with him compare?
14 Long since a God of wonders thee
    thy rescu'd people found;
15 Long since hast thou thy chosen seed,
    with strong deliv'rance crown'd.
16 When thee, O God, the waters saw,
    the frighted billows shrunk;
  The troubled depths themselves for fear
    beneath their channels sunk.
17 The clouds pour'd down, while rending skies
    did with their noise conspire;
  Thy arrows all abroad were sent,
    wing'd with avenging fire.
18 Heav'n with thy thunder's voice was torn,
    whilst all the lower world
  With light'nings blaz'd, earth shook, and seem'd
    from her foundations hurl'd.
19 Through rolling streams thou find'st thy way,
    thy paths in waters lie;
  Thy wond'rous passage, where no sight
    thy footsteps can descry.
20 Thou ledd'st thy people like a flock
    safe through the desert land,
  By Moses, their meek skilful guide,
    and Aaron's sacred hand.

PSALM LXXVIII.

1 HEAR, O my people; to my law
      devout attention lend;
  Let the instruction of my mouth
    deep in your hearts descend.
2 My tongue, by inspiration taught,
    shall parables unfold,
  Dark oracles, but understood,
    and own'd for truths of old:
  Which we from sacred registers
    of ancient times have known,
3 And our forefathers' pious care
    to us has handed down.
4 We will not hide them from our sons;
    our offspring shall be taught
  The praises of the Lord, whose strength
    has works of wonder wrought.

5 For

5 For Jacob he this law ordain'd,
    this league with Israel made;
  With charge to be from age to age,
    from race to race, convey'd.
6 That generations yet to come
    should to their unborn heirs
  Religiously transmit the same,
    and they again to theirs.
7 To teach them that in God alone
    their hope securely stands;
  That they should ne'er his works forget,
    but keep his just commands.
8 Lest, like their fathers, they might prove,
    a stiff rebellious race,
  False-hearted, fickle to their God,
    unstedfast in his grace.
9 Such were revolting Ephraim's sons,
    who, though to warfare bred,
  And skilful archers, arm'd with bows,
    from field ignobly fled.
10, 11 They falsified their league with God,
    his orders disobey'd,
  Forgot his works and miracles
    before their eyes display'd.
12 Nor wonders, which their fathers saw,
    did they in mind retain,
  Prodigious things in Egypt done;
    and Zoan's fertile plain.
13 He cut the seas to let them pass,
    restrain'd the pressing flood;
  While pil'd on heaps, on either side,
    the solid waters stood.
14 A wond'rous pillar led them on,
    compos'd of shade and light;
  A shelt'ring cloud it prov'd by day,
    a leading fire by night.
15 When drought oppress'd them, where no stream
    the wilderness supply'd,
  He cleft the rock, whose flinty breast
    dissolv'd into a tide.
16 Streams from the solid rock he brought,
    which down in rivers fell,
  That, trav'lling with their camp, each day
    renew'd the miracle.
17 Yet there they sinn'd against him more,
    provoking the Most High,
  In that same desert where he did
    their fainting souls supply.

18 They

18 They firſt incens'd him in their hearts,
    that did his power diſtruſt,
  And long'd for meat, not urg'd by want,
    but to indulge their luſt.
19 Then utter'd their blaſpheming doubts;
    " Can God," ſay they " prepare
  " A table in the wilderneſs,
  " ſet out with various fare?
20 " He ſmote the flinty rock, 'tis true,
    " and guſhing ſtreams enſu'd;
  " But can he corn and fleſh provide
    " for ſuch a multitude?"
21 The Lord with indignation heard:
    from heav'n avenging flame
  On Jacob fell, conſuming wrath
    on thankleſs Iſrael came:
22 Becauſe their unbelieving hearts
    in God would not confide,
  Nor truſt his care, who had from heav'n
    their wants ſo oft ſupply'd;
23 Though he had made his clouds diſcharge
    proviſions down in ſhow'rs;
  And when earth fail'd, reliev'd their needs
    from his celeſtial ſtores;
24 Though taſteful Manna was rain'd down,
    their hunger to relieve;
  Though from the ſtores of heav'n they did
    ſuſtaining corn receive.
25 Thus man with Angels' ſacred food,
    ingrateful man was fed;
  Not ſparingly, for ſtill they found
    a plenteous table ſpread.
26 From heav'n he made an eaſt wind blow,
    then did the ſouth command
27 To rain down fleſh like duſt, and fowls
    like ſea's unnumber'd ſand.
28 Within their trenches he let fall
    the luſcious eaſy prey;
  And all around their ſpreading camp
    the ready booty lay.
29 They fed, were fill'd; he gave them leave
    their appetites to feaſt;
30, 31 Yet ſtill their wanton luſt crav'd on,
    nor with their hunger ceas'd.
  But whilſt in their luxurious mouths,
    they did their dainties chew,
  The wrath of God ſmote down their chiefs,
    and Iſrael's choſen ſlew.

PART

PSALM LXXVIII.
PART II.

32 Yet still they sinn'd, nor would afford
 his miracles belief:
33 Therefore through fruitless travels he
 consum'd their lives in grief.
34 When some were slain, the rest return'd
 to God with early cry;
35 Own'd him the Rock of their defence,
 their Saviour, God most high.
36 But this was feign'd submission all;
 their heart their tongue bely'd;
37 Their heart was still perverse, nor would
 firm in his league abide.
38 Yet full of mercy, he forgave,
 nor did with death chastise;
 But turn'd his kindled wrath aside,
 or would not let it rise.
39 For he remember'd they were flesh,
 that could not long remain;
 A murm'ring wind, that's quickly past,
 and ne'er returns again.
40 How oft did they provoke him there,
 how oft his patience grieve,
 In that same desert, where he did
 their fainting souls relieve!
41 They tempted him by turning back,
 and wickedly repin'd,
 When Israel's God refus'd to be
 by their desires confin'd.
42 Nor call'd to mind the hand and day
 that their redemption brought;
43 His signs in Egypt, wond'rous works
 in Zoan's valley wrought.
44 He turn'd their rivers into blood,
 that man and beast forbore,
 And rather chose to die of thirst,
 than drink the putrid gore.
45 He sent devouring swarms of flies;
 hoarse frogs annoy'd their soil;
46 Locusts and catterpillars reap'd
 the harvest of their toil.
47 Their vines with batt'ring hails were broke;
 with frost the fig-tree dies;
48 Light'ning and hail made flocks and herds
 one gen'ral sacrifice.
49 He turn'd his anger loose, and set
 no time for it to cease;
 And with their plagues ill angels sent,
 their torments to increase.

50 He

PSALM LXXVIII.

50 He clear'd a paſſage for his wrath
    to ravage uncontroul'd;
  The murrain on their firſtlings ſeiz'd,
    in ev'ry field and fold.
51 The deadly peſt from beaſt to man,
    from field to city, came;
  It ſlew their heirs, their eldeſt hopes,
    through all the tents of Ham.
52 But his own tribe, like folded ſheep,
    he brought from their diſtreſs;
  And them conducted, like a flock,
    throughout the wilderneſs.
53 He led them on, and in their way
    no cauſe of fear they found;
  But march'd ſecurely through thoſe deeps,
    in which their foes were drown'd.
54 Nor ceas'd his care, till them he brought
    ſafe to his promis'd land;
  And to his holy mount, the prize
    of his victorious hand.
55 To them the outcaſt heathen's land
    he did by lot divide;
  And in their foes' abandon'd tents
    made Iſrael's tribes reſide.

PART III.

56 Yet ſtill they tempted, ſtill provok'd
    the wrath of God moſt high;
  Nor would to practiſe his commands
    their ſtubborn hearts apply;
57 But in their faithleſs fathers' ſteps
    perverſely choſe to go;
  They turn'd aſide, like arrows ſhot
    from ſome deceitful bow.
58 For him to fury they provok'd
    with altars ſet on high;
  And with their graven images
    inflam'd his jealouſy.
59 When God heard this, on Iſrael's tribes
    his wrath and hatred fell;
60 He quitted Shiloh, and the tents
    where once he choſe to dwell.
61 To vile captivity his ark,
    his glory to diſdain,
62 His people to the ſword he gave,
    nor would his wrath reſtrain.
63 Deſtructive war their ableſt youth
    untimely did confound;

No virgin was to th' altar led,
  with nuptial garlands crown'd.
64 In fight the sacrificer fell,
  the priest a victim bled;
And widows, who their death should mourn,
  themselves of grief were dead.
65 Then, as a giant rous'd from sleep,
  whom wine had throughly warm'd,
Shouts out aloud, the Lord awak'd,
  and his proud foe alarm'd.
66 He smote their host, that from the field
  a scatter'd remnant came,
With wounds imprinted on their backs
  of everlasting shame.
67 With conquest crown'd, he Joseph's tents
  and Ephraim's tribe forsook;
68 But Judah chose, and Sion's mount
  for his lov'd dwelling took.
69 His temple he erected there,
  with spires exalted high;
While deep, and fix'd, as those of earth
  the strong foundations lie.
70 His faithful servant David too
  he for his choice did own,
And from the sheepfolds him advanc'd
  to sit on Judah's throne.
71 From tending on the teeming ewes,
  he brought him forth to feed
His own inheritance, the tribes
  of Israel's chosen seed.
72 Exalted thus, the monarch prov'd
  a faithful shepherd still;
He fed them with and an upright heart,
  and guided them with skill.

PSALM LXXIX.

1 BEhold, O God, how heathen hosts
  have thy possession seiz'd!
Thy sacred house they have defil'd,
  thy holy city raz'd!
2 The mangled bodies of thy saints
  abroad unbury'd lay;
Their flesh expos'd to savage beasts,
  and rav'nous birds of prey.
3 Quite through Jerus'lem was their blood
  like common water shed;
And none were left alive to pay
  last duties to the dead.

PSALM LXXX.

4 The neighb'ring lands our small remains
    with loud reproaches wound;
  And we a laughing-stock are made
    to all the nations round.
5 How long wilt thou be angry, Lord?
    must we for ever mourn?
  Shall thy devouring jealous rage,
    like fire, for ever burn?
6 On foreign lands, that know not thee,
    thy heavy vengeance show'r;
  Those sinful kingdoms let it crush,
    that have not own'd thy pow'r.
7 For their devouring jaws have prey'd
    on Jacob's chosen race;
  And to a barren desert turn'd
    their fruitful dwelling-place.
8 O think not on our former sins,
    but speedily prevent
  The utter ruin of thy saints,
    almost with sorrow spent.
9 Thou God of our salvation, help,
    and free our souls from blame;
  So shall our pardon and defence
    exalt thy glorious Name.
10 Let infidels, that scoffing say,
    "Where is the God they boast?"
  In vengeance for thy slaughter'd saints,
    perceive thee to their cost.
11 Lord, hear the sighing pris'ner's moans,
    thy saving pow'r extend;
  Preserve the wretches doom'd to die,
    from that untimely end.
12 On them who us oppress let all
    our suff'rings be repaid;
  Make their confusion sev'n times more
    than what on us they laid.
13 So we, thy people and thy flock,
    shall ever praise thy Name;
  And with glad hearts our grateful thanks,
    from age to age proclaim.

PSALM LXXX.

1 O Israel's Shepherd, Joseph's Guide,
    our pray'rs to thee vouchsafe to hear;
  Thou that dost on the Cherubs ride,
    again in solemn state appear.
2 Behold how Benjamin expects,
    with Ephraim and Manasseh join'd,
  In our deliv'rance the effects,
    of thy resistless strength to find.

3 Do thou convert us, Lord, do thou
   the luſtre of thy face diſplay,
  And all the ills we ſuffer now,
   like ſcatter'd clouds ſhall paſs away.

4 O thou, whom heav'nly hoſts obey,
   how long ſhall thy fierce anger burn?
  How long thy ſuff'ring people pray,
   and to their pray'rs have no return?

5 When hungry, we are forc'd to drench
   our ſcanty food in floods of woe;
  When dry, our raging thirſt we quench
   with ſtreams of tears that largely flow.

6 For us the heathen nations round,
   as for a common prey, conteſt;
  Our foes with ſpiteful joys abound,
   and at our loſt condition jeſt.

7 Do thou convert us, Lord, do thou
   the luſtre of thy face diſplay,
  And all the ills we ſuffer now,
   like ſcatter'd clouds, ſhall paſs away.

PART II.

8 Thou brought'ſt a vine from Egypt's land;
   and, caſting out the heathen race,
  Did'ſt plant it with thine own right-hand,
   and firmly fix it in their place.

9 Before it thou prepar'dſt the way,
   and mad'ſt it take a laſting root,
  Which, bleſs'd with thy indulgent ray,
   o'er all the land did widely ſhoot.

10, 11 The hills were cover'd with its ſhade,
     its goodly boughs did cedars ſeem;
    Its branches to the ſea were ſpread,
     and reach'd to proud Euphrates' ſtream.

12 Why then haſt thou its hedge o'erthrown,
    which thou haſt made ſo firm and ſtrong?
   Whilſt all its grapes, defenceleſs grown,
    are pluck'd by thoſe that paſs along.

13 See how the briſtling foreſt-boar
    with dreadful fury lays it waſte;
   Hark! how the ſavage monſters roar,
    and to their helpleſs prey make haſte.

PART III.

14 To thee, O God of hoſts, we pray;
    thy wonted goodneſs, Lord, renew;
   From heav'n, thy throne, this vine ſurvey,
    and her ſad ſtate with pity view.

15 Behold the vineyard made by thee,
    which thy right-hand did guard ſo long;

And keep that branch from danger free,
  which for thyself thou mad'st so strong.
16 To wasting flames 'tis made a prey,
  and all its spreading boughs cut down;
At thy rebuke they soon decay,
  and perish at thy dreadful frown.
17 Crown thou the King with good success,
  by thy right-hand secur'd from wrong;
The Son of Man in mercy bless,
  whom for thyself thou mad'st so strong.
18 So shall we still continue free
  from whatsoe'er deserves thy blame;
And, if once more reviv'd by thee,
  will always praise thy holy Name.
19 Do thou convert us, Lord, do thou
  the lustre of thy face display,
And all the ills we suffer now,
  like scatter'd clouds, shall pass away.

PSALM LXXXI.

1 TO God, our never failing strength,
    with loud applauses sing;
  And jointly make a chearful noise
    to Jacob's awful King.
2 Compose a hymn of praise, and touch
    your instruments of joy;
  Let psalteries and pleasant harps
    your grateful skill employ.
3 Let trumpets at the great new moon
    their joyful voices raise,
  To celebrate th' appointed time,
    the solemn day of praise.
4 For this a statute was of old,
    which Jacob's God decreed;
  To be with pious care observ'd
    by Israel's chosen seed.
5 This he for a memorial fix'd,
    when, freed from Egypt's land,
  Strange nations' barb'rous speech we heard,
    but could not understand.
6 Your burden'd shoulders I reliev'd,
    (thus seems our God to say,)
  Your servile hands by me were freed,
    from lab'ring in the clay.
7 Your ancestors, with wrongs oppress'd,
    to me for aid did call;
  With pity I their suff'rings saw,
    and set them free from all.

PSALM LXXXII.

 They fought for me, and from the cloud
  in thunder I reply'd;
 At Meribah's contentious stream
  their faith and duty try'd.

PART II.

8 While I my solemn will declare,
  my chosen people, hear:
 If thou, O Israel, to my words
  wilt lend thy list'ning ear;
9 Then shall no god besides myself
  within thy coasts be found;
 Nor shalt thou worship any god
  of all the nations round.
10 The Lord thy God am I, who thee
  brought forth from Egypt's land;
 'Tis I that all thy just desires
  supply with lib'ral hand.
11 But they, my chosen race, refus'd
  to hearken to my voice;
 Nor would rebellious Israel's sons
  make me their happy choice.
12 So I, provok'd, resign'd them up,
  to ev'ry lust a prey;
 And in their own perverse designs
  permitted them to stray.
13 O that my people wisely would
  my just commandments heed!
 And Israel in my righteous ways
  with pious care proceed!
14 Then should my heavy judgments fall
  on all that them oppose,
 And my avenging hand be turn'd
  against their num'rous foes.
15 Their enemies and mine should all
  before my foot-stool bend;
 But as for them, their happy state,
  should never know an end.
16 All parts with plenty should abound;
  with finest wheat their field:
 The barren rocks, to please their taste,
  should richest honey yield.

PSALM LXXXII.

1 GOD in the great assembly stands,
  where his impartial eye
 In state surveys the earthly gods,
  and does their judgments try.

2, 3 How dare ye then unjuſtly judge,
　　or be to ſinners kind?
　　Defend the orphans and the poor;
　　let ſuch your juſtice find.
4 Protect the humble helpleſs man,
　　reduc'd to deep diſtreſs;
　　And let not him become a prey
　　to ſuch as would oppreſs.
5 They neither know, nor will they learn,
　　but blindly rove and ſtray;
　　Juſtice and truth, the world's ſupports,
　　through all the land decay.
6 Well then might God in anger ſay,
　　" I've call'd you by my Name;
　　" I've ſaid ye're gods and all ally'd
　　" to the Moſt High in fame:
7 " But ne'ertheleſs your unjuſt deeds
　　" to ſtrict account I'll call;
　　" You all ſhall die like common men,
　　" like other tyrants fall."
8 Ariſe, and thy juſt judgments, Lord,
　　throughout the earth diſplay;
　　And all the nations of the world
　　ſhall own thy righteous ſway.

PSALM LXXXIII.

1 HOLD not thy peace, O Lord our God,
　　no longer ſilent be;
　　Nor with conſenting quiet looks
　　our ruin calmly ſee.
2 For lo! the tumults of thy foes
　　o'er all the land are ſpread;
　　And thoſe, who hate thy ſaints and thee,
　　lift up their threat'ning head.
3 Againſt thy zealous people, Lord,
　　they craftily combine;
　　And to deſtroy thy choſen ſaints
　　have laid their cloſe deſign.
4 " Come let us cut them off," ſay they,
　　" their nation quite deface;
　　" That no remembrance may remain
　　" of Iſrael's hated race."
5 Thus they againſt thy people's peace
　　conſult with one conſent;
　　And diff'ring nations, jointly leagu'd,
　　their common malice vent.
6 The Iſhmaelites that dwell in tents,
　　with warlike Edom join'd,
　　And Moab's ſons, our ruin vow,
　　with Hagar's race combin'd.

7 Proud

7 Proud Ammon's offspring, Gebal too,
    with Amalek confpire;
The lords of Paleftine, and all
    the wealthy fons of Tyre.
8 All thefe the ftrong Affyrian king
    their firm ally have got;
Who with a pow'rful army aids
    th' inceftuous race of Lot.

PART II.

9 But let fuch vengeance come to them,
    as once to Midian came;
To Jabin and proud Sifera,
    at Kifhon's fatal ftream;
10 When thy right-hand their num'rous hofts
    near Endor did confound,
And left their carcafes for dung
    to feed the hungry ground.
11 Let all their mighty men the fate
    of Zeb and Oreb fhare;
As Zeba and Zalmuna, fo
    let all their princes fare.
12 Who, with the fame defign infpir'd,
    thus vainly boafting fpake,
" In firm poffeffion for ourfelves
" let us God's houfes take."
13 To ruin let them hafte, like wheels
    which downwards fwiftly move;
Like chaff before the wind, let all
    their fcatter'd forces prove.
14, 15 As flames confume dry wood, or heath,
    that on parch'd mountains grows,
So let thy fierce-purfuing wrath
    with terrors ftrike thy foes.
16, 17 Lord, fhroud their faces with difgrace,
    that they may own thy Name;
Or them confound, whofe harden'd hearts
    thy gentler means difclaim.
18 So fhall the wond'ring world confefs,
    that thou, who claim'ft alone
Jehovah's name, o'er all the earth
    haft rais'd thy lofty throne.

PSALM LXXXIV.

1 O God of Hofts, the mighty Lord,
    how lovely is the place,
Where thou, enthron'd in glory, fhow'ft
    the brightnefs of thy face!
2 My longing foul faints with defire
    to view thy bleft abode;

PSALM LXXXIV.

My panting heart and flesh cry out
   for thee, the living God.
3 The birds, more happy far than I,
   around thy temple throng;
Securely there they build, and there
   securely hatch their young.
4 O Lord of Hosts, my King and God,
   how highly blest are they,
Who in thy temple always dwell,
   and there thy praise display!
5 Thrice happy they, whose choice has thee
   their sure protection made;
Who long to tread the sacred ways
   that to thy dwelling lead!
6 Who pass through Baca's thirsty vale,
   yet no refreshment want;
Their pools are fill'd with rain, which thou
   at their request dost grant.
7 Thus they proceed from strength to strength,
   and still approach more near;
Till all on Sion's holy mount,
   before their God appear.
8 O Lord, the mighty God of Hosts,
   my just request regard:
Thou God of Jacob, let my pray'r
   be still with favour heard.
9 Behold, O God, for thou alone
   canst timely aid dispense;
On thy anointed servant look,
   be thou his strong defence.
10 For in thy courts one single day
   'tis better to attend,
Than, Lord, in any place besides
   a thousand days to spend.
Much rather in God's house will I
   the meanest office take,
Than in the wealthy tents of sin
   my pompous dwelling make.
11 For God, who is our Sun and Shield,
   will grace and glory give;
And no good thing will he withhold
   from them that justly live.
12 Thou God, whom heav'nly hosts obey,
   how highly blest is he,
Whose hope and trust, securely plac'd,
   is still repos'd on thee!

PSALM LXXXV.

1 LORD, thou haſt granted to thy land
    the favours we implor'd,
And faithful Jacob's captive race
    haſt gracioully reſtor'd.
2, 3 Thy people's ſins thou haſt forgiv'n,
    and all their guilt defac'd;
Thou haſt not let thy wrath flame on,
    nor thy fierce anger laſt.
4 O God our Saviour, all our hearts
    to thy obedience turn;
That, quench'd with our repenting tears,
    thy wrath no more may burn.
5, 6 For why ſhould'ſt thou be angry ſtill,
    and wrath ſo long retain?
Revive us, Lord, and let thy ſaints
    thy wonted comfort gain.
7 Thy gracious favour, Lord, diſplay,
    which we have long implor'd;
And, for thy wond'rous mercy's ſake,
    thy wonted aid afford.
8 God's anſwer patiently I'll wait;
    for he, with glad ſucceſs,
If they no more to folly turn,
    his mourning ſaints will bleſs.
9 To all that fear his holy Name
    his ſure ſalvation's near;
And in its former happy ſtate
    our nation ſhall appear.
10 For mercy now with truth is join'd,
    and righteouſneſs with peace,
Like kind companions, abſent long,
    with friendly arms embrace.
11, 12 Truth from the earth ſhall ſpring, whilſt heav'n
    ſhall ſtreams of juſtice pour;
And God, from whom all goodneſs flows,
    ſhall endleſs plenty ſhow'r.
13 Before him righteouſneſs ſhall march,
    and his juſt paths prepare;
Whilſt we his holy ſteps purſue
    with conſtant zeal and care.

PSALM LXXXVI.

1 TO my complaint, O Lord my God,
    thy gracious ear incline;
Hear me, diſtreſs'd, and deſtitute
    of all relief but thine.
2 Do thou, O God, preſerve my ſoul,
    that does thy Name adore;

Thy

PSALM LXXXVI.

Thy servant keep, and him, whose trust
relies on thee, restore.
3 To me, who daily thee invoke,
thy mercy, Lord, extend;
4 Refresh thy servant's soul, whose hopes
on thee alone depend.
5 Thou, Lord, art good, nor only good,
but prompt to pardon too;
Of plenteous mercy to all those
who for thy mercy sue.
6 To my repeated humble pray'r,
O Lord, attentive be;
7 When troubled, I on thee will call,
for thou wilt answer me.
8 Among the gods there's none like thee,
O Lord, alone divine!
To thee as much inferior they,
as are their works to thine.
9 Therefore their great Creator thee
the nations shall adore;
Their long-misguided pray'rs and praise
to thy bless'd Name restore.
10 All shall confess thee great, and great
the wonders thou hast done;
Confess thee God, the God supreme,
confess thee God alone.

PART II.

11 Teach me thy way, O Lord, and I
from truth shall ne'er depart;
In rev'rence to thy sacred Name
devoutly fix my heart.
12 Thee will I praise, O Lord my God,
praise thee with heart sincere;
And to thy everlasting Name
eternal trophies rear.
13 Thy boundless mercy shown to me
transcends my pow'r to tell;
For thou hast oft redeem'd my soul
from lowest depths of hell.
14 O God, the sons of pride and strife
have my destruction sought;
Regardless of thy pow'r, that oft
has my deliv'rance wrought.
15 But thou thy constant goodness didst
to my assistance bring;
Of patience, mercy, and of truth,
thou everlasting spring!

16 O bounteous Lord, thy grace and strength
   to me thy servant show;
Thy kind protection, Lord, on me,
   thine handmaid's son, bestow.
17 Some signal give, which my proud foes
   may see with shame and rage,
When thou, O Lord, for my relief
   and comfort dost engage.

PSALM LXXXVII.

1 GOD's temple crowns the holy mount;
2 the Lord there condescends to dwell;
His Sion's gates, in his account,
   our Israel's fairest tents excel.
3 Fame glorious things of thee shall sing,
   O city of th' Almighty King!
4 I'll mention Rahab with due praise,
   in Babylon's applauses join,
The fame of Ethiopia raise,
   with that of Tyre and Palestine;
And grant that some amongst them born,
   Their age and country did adorn.
5 But still of Sion I'll aver,
   that many such from her proceed;
Th' Almighty shall establish her:
6 His gen'ral list shall show, when read,
   That such a person there was born,
   And such did such an age adorn.
7 He'll Sion find with numbers fill'd
   of such as merit high renown;
For hand and voice musicians skill'd;
   and (her transcending fame to crown)
Of such she shall successions bring,
   Like water from a living spring.

PSALM LXXXVIII.

1 TO thee, my God and Saviour, I
      By day and night address my cry:
2 Vouchsafe my mournful voice to hear;
   To my distress incline thine ear.
3 For seas of trouble me invade,
   My soul draws nigh to death's cold shade:
4 Like one whose strength and hopes are fled,
   They number me among the dead:
5 Like those who, shrouded in the grave,
   From thee no more remembrance have;
6 Cast off from thy sustaining care,
   Down to the confines of despair.

PSALM LXXXIX.

7 Thy wrath has hard upon me lain,
 Afflicting me with reftlefs pain;
 Me all thy mountain waves have preft,
 Too weak, alas, to bear the leaft.
8 Remov'd from friends, I figh alone,
 In a loath'd dungeon laid, where none
 A vifit will vouchfafe to me,
 Confin'd, paft hopes of liberty.
9 My eyes from weeping never ceafe;
 They wafte, but ftill my griefs increafe;
 Yet daily, Lord, to thee I've pray'd,
 With out-ftretch'd hands invok'd thy aid.
10 Wilt thou by miracle revive
 The dead, whom thou forfook'ft alive?
 From death reftore, thy praife to fing,
 Whom thou from prifon would'ft not bring?
11 Shall the mute grave thy love confefs?
 A mould'ring tomb thy faithfulnefs?
12 Thy truth and power renown obtain
 Where darknefs and oblivion reign?
13 To thee, O Lord, I cry, forlorn;
 My pray'r prevents the early morn:
14 Why haft thou, Lord, my foul forfook,
 Nor once vouchfaf'd a gracious look?
15 Prevailing forrows bear me down,
 Which from my youth with me have grown;
 Thy terrors paft diftract my mind,
 And fears of blacker days behind.
16 Thy wrath hath burft upon my head,
 Thy terrors fill my foul with dread;
17 Environ'd as with waves combin'd,
 And for a gen'ral deluge join'd.
18 My lovers, friends, familiars, all
 Remov'd from fight, and out of call;
 To dark oblivion all retir'd,
 Dead, or at leaft to me expir'd.

PSALM LXXXIX.

1 THY mercies, Lord, fhall be my fong;
   my fong on them fhall ever dwell;
 To ages yet unborn my tongue
   thy never-failing truth fhall tell.
2 I have affirm'd, and ftill maintain,
   thy mercy fhall for ever laft;
 Thy truth that does the heav'ns fuftain,
   like them fhall ftand for ever faft.
3 Thus fpak'ft thou by thy Prophet's voice,
 " With David I a league have made;

" To

"To him, my servant, and my choice,
 "by solemn oath this grant convey'd:
4 "While earth, and seas, and skies endure,
 "thy seed shall in my sight remain;
 "To them thy throne I will ensure,
 "they shall to endless ages reign."

5 For such stupendous truth and love,
 both heav'n and earth just praises owe.
 By choirs of angels sung above,
 and by assembled saints below.

6 What Seraph of celestial birth
 to vie with Israel's God shall dare?
 Or who among the gods of earth
 with our Almighty Lord compare?

7 With rev'rence and religious dread
 his saints should to his temple press;
 His fear through all their hearts should spread,
 who his Almighty Name confess.

8 Lord God of armies, who can boast
 of strength or pow'r like thine renown'd;
 Of such a num'rous faithful host,
 as that which does thy throne surround?

9 Thou dost the lawless sea controul,
 and change the prospect of the deep;
 Thou mak'st the sleeping billows roll;
 thou mak'st the rolling billows sleep.

10 Thou brak'st in pieces Rahab's pride,
 and didst oppressing pow'r disarm;
 Thy scatter'd foes have dearly try'd
 the force of thy resistless arm.

11 In thee the sov'reign right remains
 of earth and heav'n; thee, Lord, alone
 The world, and all that it contains,
 their Maker and Preserver own.

12 The poles on which the globe does rest
 were form'd by thy creating voice;
 Tabor and Hermon, east and west,
 in thy sustaining pow'r rejoice.

13 Thy arm is mighty, strong thy hand,
 yet, Lord, thou dost with justice reign;
14 Possess'd of absolute command
 thou truth and mercy dost maintain.

15 Happy, thrice happy they, who hear
 thy sacred trumpet's joyful sound;
 Who may at festivals appear,
 with thy most glorious presence crown'd.

16 Thy saints shall always be o'erjoy'd,
 who on thy sacred Name rely;

And,

PSALM LXXXIX.

  And, in thy righteousness employ'd,
   above their foes be rais'd on high.
17 For in thy strength they shall advance,
   whose conquests from thy favour spring;
18 The Lord of hosts is our defence,
   and Israel's God our Israel's King.
19 Thus spak'st thou by thy Prophet's voice,
  " A mighty champion I will send;
 " From Judah's tribe have I made choice
  " of one, who shall the rest defend.
20 " My servant David I have found,
  " with holy oil anointed him;
21 " Him shall the hand support, that crown'd,
  " and guard, that gave the diadem.
22 " No prince from him shall tribute force,
  " no son of strife shall him annoy;
23 " His spiteful foes I will disperse,
  " and them before his face destroy.
24 " My truth and grace shall him sustain;
  " his armies, in well-order'd ranks,
25 " Shall conquer, from the Tyrian Main
  " to Tigris and Euphrates' banks.
26 " Me for his Father he shall take,
  " his God and Rock of safety call;
27 " Him I my first-born son will make,
  " and earthly kings his subjects all.
28 " To him my mercy I'll secure,
  " my cov'nant make for ever fast:
29 " His seed for ever shall endure;
  " his throne, till heav'n dissolves, shall last.

PART II.

30 " But if his heirs my law forsake,
  " and from my sacred precepts stray;
31 " If they my righteous statutes break,
  " nor strictly my commands obey;
32 " Their sins I'll visit with a rod,
  " and for their folly make them smart;
33 " Yet will not cease to be their God,
  " nor from my truth, like them, depart.
34 " My cov'nant I will ne'er revoke,
  " but in remembrance fast retain;
 " The thing that once my lips have spoke
  " shall in eternal force remain.
35 " Once I have sworn, but once for all,
  " and made my holiness the tie,
 " That I my grant will ne'er recall,
  " nor to my servant David lie:

36 "Whose throne and race the constant sun
"shall, like his course, establish'd see;
37 "Of this my oath, thou conscious moon,
"in heav'n, my faithful witness be."
38 Such was thy gracious promise, Lord;
but thou hast now our tribes forsook,
Thy own anointed hast abhor'd,
and turn'd on him thy wrathful look:
39 Thou seemest to have render'd void
the cov'nant with thy servant made;
Thou hast his dignity destroy'd,
and in the dust his honour laid.
40 Of strong holds thou hast him bereft,
and brought his bulwarks to decay;
41 His frontier coasts defenceless left,
a public scorn, and common prey.
42 His ruin does glad triumphs yield
to foes, advanc'd by thee to might;
43 Thou hast his conqu'ring sword unsteel'd,
his valour turn'd to shameful flight.
44 His glory is to darkness fled,
his throne is levell'd with the ground;
45 His youth to wretched bondage led,
with shame o'erwhelm'd and sorrow drown'd.
46 How long shall we thy absence mourn?
wilt thou for ever, Lord, retire?
Shall thy consuming anger burn,
till that and we at once expire?
47 Consider, Lord, how short a space
thou dost for mortal life ordain;
No method to prolong the race,
but loading it with grief and pain.
48 What man is he that can controul
death's strict unalterable doom?
Or rescue from the grave his soul,
the grave that must mankind intomb?
49 Lord, where's thy love, thy boundless grace,
the oath to which thy truth did seal,
Consign'd to David and his race,
the grant which time should ne'er repeal?
50 See how thy servants treated are
with infamy, reproach and spite;
Which in my silent breast I bear,
from nations of licentious might.
51 How they, reproaching thy great Name,
have made thy servant's hope their jest;
52 Yet thy just praises we'll proclaim,
and ever sing, The Lord be blest.

PSALM

PSALM XC.

1 O Lord, the Saviour and defence
   of us thy chosen race,
From age to age thou still hast been
   our sure abiding place.
2 Before thou brought'st the mountains forth,
   or th' earth and world didst frame,
Thou always wast the mighty God,
   and ever art the same.
3 Thou turnest man, O Lord, to dust,
   of which he first was made;
And when thou speak'st the word, Return,
   'tis instantly obey'd.
4 For in thy sight a thousand years
   are like a day that's past,
Or like a watch in dead of night,
   whose hours unminded waste.
5 Thou sweep'st us off as with a flood,
   we vanish hence like dreams;
At first we grow like grass, that feels
   the sun's reviving beams:
6 But howsoever fresh and fair
   its morning beauty shows;
'Tis all cut down and wither'd quite,
   before the ev'ning close.
7, 8 We by thine anger are consum'd,
   and by thy wrath dismay'd;
Our public crimes and secret sins
   before thy sight are laid.
9 Beneath thy anger's sad effects
   our drooping days we spend;
Our unregarded years break off,
   like tales that quickly end.
10 Our term of time is sev'nty years,
   an age that few survive;
But if, with more than common strength,
   to eighty we arrive,
Yet then our boasted strength decays,
   to sorrow turn'd and pain;
So soon the slender thread is cut,
   and we no more remain.

PART II.

11 But who thy anger's dread effects
   does, as he ought, revere?
And yet thy wrath does fall or rise,
   as more or less we fear.
12 So teach us, Lord, th' uncertain sum
   of our short days to mind,

That to true wisdom all our hearts
    may ever be inclin'd.
13 O to thy servants, Lord, return,
    and speedily relent!
As we forsake our sins, do thou
    revoke our punishment.
14 To satisfy and cheer our souls,
    thy early mercy send;
That we may all our days to come
    in joy and comfort spend.
15 Let happy times, with large amends,
    dry up our former tears,
Or equal at the least the term
    of our afflicted years.
16 To all thy servants, Lord, let this
    thy wond'rous work be known,
And to our offspring yet unborn
    thy glorious pow'r be shown.
17 Let thy bright rays upon us shine,
    give thou our work success;
The glorious work we have in hand
    do thou vouchsafe to bless.

PSALM XCI.

1 HE that has God his guardian made,
    Shall, under the Almighty's shade,
    secure and undisturb'd abide:
2 Thus to my soul of him I'll say,
    He is my fortress and my stay,
    my God, in whom I will confide.
3 His tender love and watchful care
Shall free thee from the fowler's snare,
    and from the noisome pestilence:
4 He over thee his wings shall spread,
And cover thy unguarded head;
    his truth shall be thy strong defence.
5 No terrors that surprise by night
Shall thy undaunted courage fright,
    nor deadly shafts that fly by day;
6 Nor plague, of unknown rise, that kills
In darkness, nor infectious ills
    that in the hottest season slay.
7 A thousand at thy side shall die,
At thy right-hand ten thousand lie,
    while thy firm health untouch'd remains;
8 Thou only shalt look on and see
The wicked's dismal tragedy,
    and count the sinner's mournful gains.

PSALM XCII.

9 Becaufe, with well-plac'd confidence,
Thou mak'ſt the Lord thy ſure defence,
　and on the Higheſt doth rely;
10 Therefore no ill ſhall thee befall,
Nor to thy healthful dwelling ſhall
　any infectious plagues draw nigh.
11 For he throughout thy happy days,
To keep thee ſafe in all thy ways,
　ſhall give his angels ſtrict commands;
12 And they, leſt thou ſhould'ſt chance to meet
With ſome rough ſtone to wound thy feet,
　ſhall bear thee ſafely in their hands.
13 Dragons and aſps that thirſt for blood,
And lions roaring for their food,
　beneath his conqu'ring feet ſhall lie:
14 Becauſe he lov'd and honour'd me,
Therefore, ſays God, I'll ſet him free,
　and fix his glorious throne on high.
15 He'll call; I'll anſwer when he calls,
And reſcue him when ill befalls;
　increaſe his honour and his wealth:
16 And when, with undiſturb'd content,
His long and happy life is ſpent,
　his end I'll crown with ſaving health.

PSALM XCII.

1 HOW good and pleaſant muſt it be
　　to thank the Lord moſt high;
And with repeated hymns of praiſe
　his Name to magnify!
2 With ev'ry morning's early dawn
　his goodneſs to relate;
And of his conſtant truth, each night,
　the glad effects repeat!
3 To ten-ſtring'd inſtruments we'll ſing,
　with tuneful pſalt'ries join'd;
And to the harp, with ſolemn ſounds,
　for ſacred uſe deſign'd.
4 For through thy wond'rous works, O Lord,
　thou mak'ſt my heart rejoice;
The thoughts of them ſhall make me glad,
　and ſhout with chearful voice.
5, 6 How wond'rous are thy works, O Lord!
　how deep are thy decrees!
Whoſe winding tracks, in ſecret laid,
　no ſtupid ſinner ſees.
7 He little thinks, when wicked men,
　like graſs, look freſh and gay,

How soon their short-liv'd splendour must
  for ever pass away.
8, 9 But thou, my God, art still most high;
  and all thy lofty foes,
Who thought they might securely sin,
  shall be o'erwhelm'd with woes.
10 Whilst thou exalt'st my sov'reign pow'r,
  and mak'st it largely spread;
And with refreshing oil anoint'st
  my consecrated head.
11 I soon shall see my stubborn foes
  to utter ruin brought;
And hear the dismal end of those,
  who have against me fought.
12 But righteous men, like fruitful palms,
  shall make a glorious show;
As cedars that on Lebanon
  in stately order grow.
13, 14 These, planted in the house of God,
  within his courts shall thrive;
Their vigour and their lustre both
  shall in old age revive.
15 Thus will the Lord his justice show;
  and God, my strong defence,
Shall due rewards to all the world
  impartially dispense.

PSALM XCIII.

1 WITH glory clad, with strength array'd,
    the Lord, that o'er all nature reigns,
The world's foundation strongly laid,
  and the vast fabric still sustains.
2 How surely 'stablish'd is thy throne,
  which shall no change or period see!
For thou, O Lord, and thou alone,
  art God from all eternity!
3, 4 The floods, O Lord, lift up their voice,
  and toss the troubled waves on high;
But God above can still their noise,
  and make the angry sea comply.
5 Thy promise, Lord, is ever sure;
  and they that in thy house would dwell,
That happy station to secure,
  must still in holiness excel.

PSALM XCIV.

1, 2 O God, to whom revenge belongs,
      thy vengeance now disclose;
Arise, thou Judge of all the earth,
  and crush thy haughty foes.

PSALM XCIV.

3, 4 How long, O Lord, shall sinful men
    their solemn triumphs make?
How long their wicked actions boast,
    and insolently speak?
5, 6 Not only they thy saints oppress,
    but, unprovok'd, they spill
The widow's and the stranger's blood,
    and helpless orphans kill.
7 "And yet the Lord shall ne'er perceive,"
    profanely thus they speak,
" Nor any notice of our deeds
" the God of Jacob take."
8 At length, ye stupid fools, your wants
    endeavour to discern:
In folly will you still proceed,
    and wisdom never learn?
9, 10 Can he be deaf who form'd the ear?
    or blind, who fram'd the eye?
Shall earth's great Judge not punish those,
    who his known will defy?
11 He fathoms all the thoughts of men;
    to him their hearts lie bare;
His eye surveys them all, and sees
    how vain their counsels are.

PART II.

12 Bless'd is the man, whom thou, O Lord,
    in kindness dost chastise;
And by thy sacred rules to walk
    dost lovingly advise.
13 This man shall rest and safety find
    in seasons of distress;
Whilst God prepares a pit for those,
    that stubbornly transgress.
14 For God will never from his saints
    his favour wholly take;
His own possession and his lot
    he will not quite forsake.
15 The world shall then confess thee just
    in all that thou hast done;
And those that choose thy upright ways,
    shall in those paths go on.
16 Who will appear in my behalf,
    when wicked men invade?
Or who, when sinners would oppress,
    my righteous cause shall plead?
17, 18, 19 Long since had I in silence slept,
    but that the Lord was near,
To stay me when I slipt; when sad,
    my troubled heart to cheer.

20 Wilt thou, who art a God most just,
 their sinful throne sustain,
 Who make the law a fair pretence
 their wicked ends to gain?
21 Against the lives of righteous men
 they form their close design;
 And blood of innocents to spill
 in solemn league combine.
22 But my defence is firmly plac'd
 in God, the Lord most high:
 He is my rock, to which I may
 for refuge always fly.
23 The Lord shall cause their ill designs
 on their own heads to fall:
 He in their sins shall cut them off,
 our God shall slay them all.

PSALM XCV.

1 O Come, loud anthems let us sing,
 Loud thanks to our Almighty King;
 For we our voices high should raise,
 When our salvation's Rock we praise.
2 Into his presence let us haste,
 To thank him for his favours past;
 To him address, in joyful songs,
 The praise that to his Name belongs.
3 For God the Lord, enthron'd in state,
 Is, with unrivall'd glory, great:
 A King superior far to all,
 Whom gods the heathen falsely call.
4 The depths of earth are in his hand,
 Her secret wealth at his command,
 The strength of hills that reach the skies,
 Subjected to his empire lies.
5 The rolling ocean's vast abyss,
 By the same sov'reign right, is his;
 'Tis mov'd by his Almighty Hand,
 That form'd and fix'd the solid land.
6 O let us to his courts repair,
 And bow with adoration there;
 Down on our knees devoutly all!
 Before the Lord, our Maker, fall.
7 For he's our God, our Shepherd he,
 His flock and pasture sheep are we:
 If then you'll, like his flock, draw near,
 To day if you his voice will hear,
8 Let not your harden'd hearts renew
 Your fathers' crimes and judgments too;

Nor here provoke my wrath, as they
In desert plains of Meribah.
9 When through the wilderness they mov'd,
And me with fresh temptations prov'd,
They still, through unbelief, rebell'd,
Whilst they my wond'rous works beheld.
10 They forty years my patience griev'd,
Though daily I their wants reliev'd.
Then—'Tis a faithless race, I said,
Whose heart from me has always stray'd.
11 They ne'er will tread my righteous path;
Therefore to them, in settled wrath,
Since they despis'd my rest, I sware,
That they should never enter there.

PSALM XCVI.

1 SING to the Lord a new-made song;
Let earth in one assembled throng
her common Patron's praise resound:
2 Sing to the Lord, and bless his Name,
From day to day his praise proclaim,
who us has with salvation crown'd:
3 To heathen lands his fame rehearse,
His wonders to the universe.
4 He's great, and greatly to be prais'd;
In majesty and glory rais'd
above all other deities:
5 For pageantry and idols all
Are they, whom gods the heathen call;
he only rules, who made the skies:
6 With majesty and honour crown'd,
Beauty and strength his throne surround.
7 Be therefore both to him restor'd
By you, who have false gods ador'd;
ascribe due honour to his Name:
8 Peace-off'rings on his altar lay,
Before his throne your homage pay,
which he, and he alone, can claim:
9 To worship at his sacred court,
Let all the trembling world resort.
10 Proclaim aloud, Jehovah reigns,
Whose pow'r the universe sustains,
and banish'd justice will restore;
11 Let therefore heav'n new joys confess;
And heav'nly mirth let earth express;
its loud applause the ocean roar;
Its mute inhabitants rejoice,
And for this triumph find a voice.

12 For joy let fertile vallies sing,
   The chearful groves their tribute bring,
      the tuneful choir of birds awake,
13 The Lord's approach to celebrate;
   Who now sets out with awful state,
      his circuit through the earth to take:
   From heav'n to judge the world he's come,
   With justice to reward and doom.

PSALM XCVII.

1 Jehovah reigns, let all the earth
      in his just government rejoice;
   Let all the isles with sacred mirth,
      in his applause unite their voice.
2 Darkness and clouds of awful shade
      his dazzling glory shroud in state;
   Justice and truth his guards are made,
      and fix'd by his pavilion wait.
3 Devouring fire before his face,
      his foes around with vengeance struck;
4 His light'ning set the world on blaze;
      earth saw it, and with terror shook.
5 The proudest hills his presence felt,
      their height nor strength could help afford;
   The proudest hills like wax did melt
      in presence of th' Almighty Lord.
6 The heav'ns, his righteousness to show,
      with storms of fire our foes pursu'd,
   And all the trembling world below
      have his descending glory view'd.
7 Confounded be their impious host,
      who make the gods to whom they pray;
   All who of pageant idols boast:
      to him, ye gods, your worship pay.
8 Glad Sion of thy triumph heard,
      and Judah's daughters were o'erjoy'd;
   Because thy righteous judgments, Lord,
      have pagan pride and pow'r destroy'd.
9 For thou, O God, art seated high,
      above earth's potentates enthron'd;
   Thou, Lord, unrivall'd in the sky,
      supreme by all the gods art own'd.
10 Ye who to serve this Lord aspire,
      abhor what's ill, and truth esteem:
   He'll keep his servants' souls entire,
      and them from wicked hands redeem.
11 For seeds are sown of glorious light,
      a future harvest for the just;
   And gladness for the heart that's right,
      to recompense its pious trust.

12 Rejoice, ye righteous, in the Lord;
   memorials of his holiness
Deep in your faithful breasts record,
   and with your thankful tongues confess.

PSALM XCVIII.

1 SING to the Lord a new-made song,
    who wond'rous things has done;
  With his right-hand and holy arm
    the conquest he has won.
2 The Lord has through th' astonish'd world
    display'd his saving might,
  And made his righteous acts appear
    in all the heathen's sight.
3 Of Israel's house his love and truth
    have ever mindful been;
  Wide earth's remotest parts the pow'r
    of Israel's God have seen.
4 Let therefore earth's inhabitants
    their chearful voices raise;
  And all, with universal joy,
    resound their Maker's praise.
5 With harp and hymn's soft melody,
    into the concert bring
6 The trumpet and shrill cornet's sound,
    before th' Almighty King.
7 Let the loud ocean roar her joy,
    with all the seas contain;
  The earth, and her inhabitants,
    join concert with the main.
8 With joy let riv'lets swell to streams,
    to spreading torrents they;
  And echoing vales from hill to hill
    redoubled shouts convey;
9 To welcome down the world's great Judge,
    who does with justice come,
  And with impartial equity,
    both to reward and doom.

PSALM XCIX.

1 JEhovah reigns; let therefore all
    the guilty nations quake:
  On Cherubs' wings he sits enthron'd;
    let earth's foundations shake.
2 On Sion's hill he keeps his court,
    his palace makes her tow'rs;
  Yet thence his sov'reignty extends
    supreme o'er earthly pow'rs.
3 Let therefore all with praise address
    his great and dreadful Name;

And,

PSALM C.

And, with his unresisted might,
  his holiness proclaim.
4 For truth and justice, in his reign,
  of strength and pow'r take place;
  His judgments are with righteousness
  dispens'd to Jacob's race.
5 Therefore exalt the Lord our God;
  before his foot-stool fall;
  And, with his unresisted might,
  his holiness extol.
6 Moses and Aaron thus of old
  among his priests ador'd;
  Among his prophets Samuel thus
  his sacred Name implor'd.
  Distress'd, upon the Lord they call'd,
  who ne'er their suit deny'd;
  But, as with rev'rence they implor'd,
  he graciously reply'd.
7 For with their camp, to guide their march,
  the cloudy pillar mov'd;
  They kept his law, and to his will
  obedient servants prov'd.
8 He answered them, forgiving oft
  his people for their sake;
  And those who rashly them oppos'd,
  did sad examples make.
9 With worship at his sacred courts
  exalt our God and Lord;
  For he, who only holy is,
  alone should be ador'd.

PSALM C.

1, 2 WITH one consent, let all the earth
  to God their chearful voices raise;
  Glad homage pay, with awful mirth,
  and sing before him songs of praise:
3 Convinc'd that he is God alone,
  from whom both we and all proceed;
  We, whom he chooses for his own,
  the flock that he vouchsafes to feed.
4 O enter then his temple gate,
  thence to his courts devoutly press;
  And still your grateful hymns repeat,
  and still his Name with praises bless.
5 For he's the Lord, supremely good,
  his mercy is for ever sure;
  His truth, which always firmly stood,
  to endless ages shall endure.

PSALM CI.

1 OF mercy's never-failing spring,
   And stedfast judgment, I will sing:
   And, since they both to thee belong,
   To thee, O Lord, address my song.
2 When, Lord, thou shalt with me reside,
   Wise discipline my reign shall guide;
   With blameless life myself I'll make
   A pattern for my court to take.
3 No ill design will I pursue,
   Nor those my fav'rites make that do:
4 Who to reproof has no regard,
   Him will I totally discard.
5 The private slanderer shall be
   In public justice doom'd by me:
   From haughty looks I'll turn aside,
   And mortify the heart of pride.
6 But honesty, call'd from her cell,
   In splendor at my court shall dwell:
   Who virtue's practice make their care,
   Shall have the first preferments there.
7 No politics shall recommend
   His country's foe to be my friend:
   None e'er shall to my favour rise,
   By flatt'ring or malicious lies.
8 All those who wicked courses take,
   An early sacrifice I'll make;
   Cut off, destroy, till none remain
   God's holy city to profane.

PSALM CII.

1 WHEN I pour out my soul in pray'r,
     do thou, O Lord, attend;
   To thy eternal throne of grace
     let my sad cry ascend.
2 O hide not thou thy glorious face
     in times of deep distress:
   Incline thine ear, and when I call,
     my sorrows soon redress.
3 Each cloudy portion of my life,
     like scatter'd smoke expires;
   My shrivell'd bones are like a hearth
     parch'd with continual fires.
4 My heart, like grass that feels the blast
     of some infectious wind,
   Does languish so with grief, that scarce
     my needful food I mind.
5 By reason of my sad estate
     I spend my breath in groans;

PSALM CII.

My flesh is worn away, my skin
    scarce hides my starting bones.
6 I'm like a pelican become,
    that does in deserts mourn;
Or like an owl, that sits all day
    on barren trees forlorn.
7 In watchings, or in restless dreams,
    the night by me is spent,
As by those solitary birds,
    that lonesome roofs frequent.
8 All day by railing foes I'm made
    the subject of their scorn;
Who all, possess'd with furious rage,
    have my destruction sworn.
9 When grov'ling on the ground I lie,
    oppress'd with grief and fears,
My bread is strew'd with ashes o'er,
    my drink is mix'd with tears.
10 Because on me with double weight
    thy heavy wrath doth lie;
For thou, to make my fall more great,
    didst lift me up on high.
11 My days, just hast'ning to their end,
    are like an ev'ning shade;
My beauty does, like wither'd grass,
    with waning lustre fade.
12 But thy eternal state, O Lord,
    no length of time shall waste;
The mem'ry of thy wond'rous works
    from age to age shall last.
13 Thou shalt arise, and Sion view
    with an unclouded face;
For now her time is come, thy own
    appointed day of grace.
14 Her scatter'd ruins by thy saints
    with pity are survey'd;
They grieve to see her lofty spires
    in dust and rubbish laid.
15, 16 The Name and glory of the Lord
    all heathen kings shall fear;
When he shall Sion build again,
    and in full state appear.
17, 18 When he regards the poor's request,
    nor slights their earnest pray'r;
Our sons, for their recorded grace,
    shall his just praise declare.
19 For God, from his abode on high,
    his gracious beams display'd:

PSALM CIII.

The Lord, from heav'n, his lofty throne,
    hath all the earth survey'd.
20 He listen'd to the captives' moans,
    he heard their mournful cry,
And freed, by his resistless pow'r,
    the wretches doom'd to die.
21 That they in Sion, where he dwells,
    might celebrate his fame,
And through the holy city sing
    loud praises to his Name:
22 When all the tribes assembling there,
    their solemn vows address,
And neighb'ring lands, with glad consent,
    the Lord their God confess.
23 But e'er my race is run, my strength
    through his fierce wrath decays;
He has, when all my wishes bloom'd,
    cut short my hopeful days.
24 Lord, end not thou my life, said I,
    when half is scarcely past;
Thy years, from worldly changes free,
    to endless ages last.
25 The strong foundations of the earth
    of old by thee were laid;
Thy hands the beauteous arch of heav'n
    with wond'rous skill have made.
26, 27 Whilst thou for ever shalt endure,
    they soon shall pass away;
And, like a garment often worn,
    shall tarnish and decay.

Like that, when thou ordain'st their change,
    to thy command they bend;
But thou continu'st still the same,
    nor have thy years an end.
28 Thou to the children of thy saints
    shalt lasting quiet give;
Whose happy race, securely fix'd,
    shall in thy presence live.

PSALM CIII.

1, 2 MY soul, inspir'd with sacred love,
    God's holy Name for ever bless;
Of all his favours mindful prove,
    and still thy grateful thanks express.
3, 4 'Tis he that all thy sins forgives,
    and after sickness makes thee sound;
From danger he thy life retrieves,
    by him with grace and mercy crown'd.

5, 6 He with good things thy mouth supplies,
   thy vigour, eagle-like, renews:
He, when the guiltless suff'rer cries,
   his foe with just revenge pursues.
7 God made of old his righteous ways
   to Moses and our fathers known;
His works, to his eternal praise,
   were to the sons of Jacob shown.
8 The Lord abounds with tender love,
   and unexampled acts of grace;
His waken'd wrath doth slowly move,
   his willing mercy flies apace.
9, 10 God will not always harshly chide,
   but with his anger quickly part;
And loves his punishments to guide
   more by his love than our desert.
11 As high as heav'n its arch extends
   above this little spot of clay,
So much his boundless love transcends
   the small respects that we can pay.
12, 13 As far as 'tis from east to west,
   so far has he our sins remov'd;
Who, with a father's tender breast,
   has such as fear him always lov'd.
14, 15 For God, who all our frame surveys,
   considers that we are but clay;
How fresh so'er we seem, our days
   like grass or flow'rs must fade away.
16, 17 Whilst they are nipt with sudden blasts,
   nor can we find their former place;
God's faithful mercy ever lasts,
   to those that fear him, and their race.
18 This shall attend on such as still
   proceed in his appointed way;
And who not only know his will,
   but to it just obedience pay.
19, 20 The Lord, the universal king,
   in heav'n has fix'd his lofty throne:
To him, ye Angels, praises sing,
   in whose great strength his pow'r is shown,
Ye that his just commands obey,
   and hear and do his sacred will,
21 Ye hosts of his, this tribute pay,
   who still what he ordains fulfil.
22 Let ev'ry creature jointly bless
   the mighty Lord: and thou, my heart,
With grateful joy thy thanks express,
   and in this concert bear thy part.

PSALM CIV.

1 BLESS God, my soul: thou, Lord, alone
    possessest empire without bounds;
  With honour thou art crown'd, thy throne
    eternal Majesty surrounds.
2 With light thou dost thyself enrobe,
    and glory for a garment take;
  Heav'n's curtains stretch beyond the globe,
    thy canopy of state to make.
3 God builds on liquid air, and forms
    his palace chambers in the skies;
  The clouds his chariots are, and storms
    the swift-wing'd steeds with which he flies.
4 As bright as flame, as swift as wind,
    his ministers heav'n's palace fill,
  To have their sundry tasks assign'd,
    all proud to serve their Sov'reign's will.
5, 6 Earth on her centre fix'd, he set,
    her face with waters overspread;
  Nor proudest mountains dar'd as yet
    to lift above the waves their head.
7 But when thy awful face appear'd,
    th' insulting waves dispers'd; they fled,
  When once thy thunder's voice they heard,
    and by their haste confess'd their dread.
8 Thence up by secret tracks they creep,
    and, gushing from the mountain's side,
  Through valleys travel to the deep,
    appointed to receive their tide.
9 There hast thou fix'd the ocean's bounds,
    the threat'ning surges to repel;
  That they no more o'erpass their mounds,
    nor to a second deluge swell.

PART II.

10 Yet thence in smaller parties drawn,
     the sea recovers her lost hills;
   And starting springs from ev'ry lawn
     surprise the vales with plenteous rills.
11 The fields' tame beasts are thither led,
     weary with labour, faint with drought;
   And asses on wild mountains bred
     have sense to find these currents out.
12 Their shady trees from scorching beams
     yield shelter to the feather'd throng;
   They drink, and to the bounteous streams
     return the tribute of their song.
13 His rains from heav'n parch'd hills recruit,
     that soon transmit the liquid store;

Till earth is burden'd with her fruit,
    and nature's lap can hold no more.
14 Grafs, for our cattle to devour,
    he makes the growth of ev'ry field:
  Herbs, for man's ufe, of various pow'r,
    that either food or phyfic yield.
15 With clufter'd grapes he crowns the vine,
    to cheer man's heart, opprefs'd with cares;
  Gives oil, that makes his face to fhine,
    and corn, that wafted ftrength repairs.

PART III.

16 The trees of God, without the care
    or art of man, with fap are fed:
  The mountain cedar looks as fair
    as thofe in royal gardens bred.
17 Safe in the lofty cedar's arms
    the wand'rers of the air may reft;
  The hofpitable pine from harms
    protects the ftork, her pious gueft.
18 Wild goats the craggy rock afcend,
    its tow'ring heights their fortrefs make,
  Whofe cells in labyrinths extend,
    where feebler creatures refuge take.
19 The moon's inconftant afpect fhows
    th' appointed feafons of the year;
  Th' inftructed fun his duty knows,
    his hours to rife and difappear.
20, 21 Darknefs he makes the earth to fhroud,
    when foreft beafts fecurely ftray;
  Young lions roar their wants aloud
    to Providence, that fends them prey.
22 They range all night, on flaughter bent,
    till fummon'd by the rifing morn,
  To fkulk in dens, with one confent
    the confcious ravagers return.
23 Forth to the tillage of his foil
    the hufbandman fecurely goes,
  Commencing with the fun his toil,
    with him returns to his repofe.
24 How various, Lord, thy works are found;
    for which thy wifdom we adore!
  The earth is with thy treafure crown'd,
    till nature's hand can grafp no more.

PART IV.

25 But ftill the vaft unfathom'd main,
    of wonders a new fcene fupplies,
  Whofe depths inhabitants contain
    of ev'ry form, and ev'ry fize.

26 Full-freighted ships from ev'ry port
   there cut their unmolested way;
Leviathan, whom there to sport
   thou mad'st, has compass there to play.
27 These various troops of sea and land
   in sense of common want agree;
All wait on thy dispensing hand,
   and have their daily alms from thee.
28 They gather what thy stores disperse,
   without their trouble to provide;
Thou op'st thy hand, the universe,
   the craving world, is all supply'd.
29 Thou for a moment hid'st thy face,
   the num'rous ranks of creatures mourn;
Thou tak'st their breath, all nature's race
   forthwith to mother earth return.
30 Again thou send'st thy spirit forth
   t' inspire the mass with vital seed;
Nature's restor'd, and parent earth
   smiles on her new-created breed.
31 Thus through successive ages stands
   firm fix'd thy providential care;
Pleas'd with the work of thy own hands,
   thou dost the waste of time repair.
32 One look of thine, one wrathful look,
   earth's panting breast with terror fills;
One touch from thee, with clouds of smoke
   in darkness shrouds the proudest hills.
33 In praising God, while he prolongs
   my breath, I will that breath employ;
34 And join devotion to my songs,
   sincere, as in him is my joy.
35 While sinners from earth's face are hurl'd,
   my soul, praise thou his holy Name,
Till with my song the list'ning world
   join concert, and his praise proclaim.

PSALM CV.

1 O Render thanks, and bless the Lord;
     invoke his sacred Name;
Acquaint the nations with his deeds,
   his matchless deeds proclaim.
2 Sing to his praise in lofty hymns;
   his wond'rous works rehearse;
Make them the theme of your discourse,
   and subject of your verse.
3 Rejoice in his Almighty Name;
   alone to be ador'd;
And let their hearts o'erflow with joy
   that humbly seek the Lord.

PSALM CV.

4 Seek ye the Lord, his saving strength
   devoutly still implore;
And, where he's ever present, seek
   his face for evermore.

5 The wonders that his hands have wrought
   keep thankfully in mind;
The righteous statutes of his mouth,
   and laws to us assign'd.

6 Know ye his servant Abra'm's seed,
   and Jacob's chosen race;

7 He's still our God, his judgments still
   throughout the earth take place.

8 His cov'nant he hath kept in mind
   for num'rous ages past,
Which yet for thousand ages more
   in equal force shall last.

9 First sign'd to Abra'm, next, by oath
   to Isaac made secure;

10 To Jacob and his heirs a law,
   for ever to endure:

11 That Canaan's land should be their lot,
   when yet but few they were;

12 But few in number, and those few
   all friendless strangers there.

13 In pilgrimage, from realm to realm,
   securely they remov'd;

14 Whilst proudest monarchs, for their sakes
   severely he reprov'd.

15 "These mine anointed are," said he;
   "let none my servants wrong;
"Nor treat the poorest prophet ill,
   "that does to me belong."

16 A dearth at last, by his command,
   did through the land prevail;
Till corn, the chief support of life,
   sustaining corn, did fail.

17 But his indulgent providence,
   had pious Joseph sent,
Sold into Egypt, but their death,
   who sold him to prevent.

18 His feet with heavy chains were crush'd,
   with calumny his fame;

19 Till God's appointed time and word
   to his deliv'rance came.

20 The king his sov'reign order sent,
   and rescu'd him with speed;
Whom private malice had confin'd,
   the peoples' ruler freed.

PSALM CV.

21 His court, revenues, realms, were all
    subjected to his will;
22 His greatest princes to controul,
    and teach his statesmen skill.

PART II.

23 To Egypt then, invited guests,
    half-famish'd Israel came;
    And Jacob held, by royal grant,
    the fertile soil of Ham.
24 Th' Almighty there with such increase
    his people multiply'd,
    Till with their proud oppressors they
    in strength and number vy'd.
25 Their vast increase th' Egyptians' hearts
    with jealous anger fir'd,
    Till they his servants to destroy
    by treach'rous arts conspir'd.
26 His servant Moses then he sent,
    his chosen Aaron too,
27 Empower'd with signs and miracles,
    to prove their mission true.
28 He call'd for darkness, darkness came,
    nature his summons knew;
29 Each stream and lake, transform'd to blood,
    the wand'ring fishes slew.
30 In putrid floods, throughout the land,
    the pest of frogs was bred;
    From noisome fens sent up to croak
    at Pharoah's board and bed.
31 He gave the sign, and swarms of flies
    came down in cloudy hosts;
    Whilst earth's enliven'd dust below,
    bred lice through all their coasts.
32 He sent them batt'ring hail for rain,
    and fire for cooling dew;
33 He smote their vines, and forest plants,
    and garden's pride o'erthrew.
34 He spake the word, and locusts came,
    and catterpillars join'd;
    They prey'd upon the poor remains
    the storm had left behind.
35 From trees to herbage they descend,
    no verdant thing they spare;
    But, like the naked fallow field,
    leave all the pastures bare.
36 From fields to villages and towns,
    commission'd vengeance flew;
    One fatal stroke their eldest hopes
    and strength of Egypt slew.

37 He

37 He brought his servants forth, enrich'd
    with Egypt's borrow'd wealth;
  And, what transcends all treasure else,
    enrich'd with vig'rous health.
38 Egypt rejoic'd, in hopes to find
    her plagues with them remov'd;
  Taught dearly now to fear worse ills
    by those already prov'd.
39 Their shrouding canopy by day
    a journeying cloud was spread;
  A fiery pillar all the night
    their desert marches led.
40 They long'd for flesh; with ev'ning quails
    he furnish'd ev'ry tent;
  From heav'n's high granery, each morn,
    the bread of Angels sent.
41 He smote the rock, whose flinty breast
    pour'd forth a gushing tide;
  Whose flowing stream, where'er they march'd,
    the desert's drought supply'd.
42 For still he did on Abra'm's faith
    and ancient league reflect;
43 He brought his people forth with joy,
    with triumph his elect.
44 Quite rooting out their heathen foes
    from Canaan's fertile soil,
  To them in cheap possession gave
    the fruit of others' toil:
45 That they his statutes might observe,
    his sacred laws obey:
  For benefits so vast, let us
    our songs of praise repay.

PSALM CVI.

1 O Render thanks to God above,
    The Fountain of eternal love;
  Whose mercy firm through ages past
  Has stood, and shall for ever last.
2 Who can his mighty deeds express,
  Not only vast, but numberless?
  What mortal eloquence can raise
  His tribute of immortal praise?
3 Happy are they, and only they,
  Who from thy judgments never stray:
  Who know what's right; nor only so,
  But always practise what they know.
4 Extend to me that favour, Lord,
  Thou to thy chosen dost afford!
  When thou return'st to set them free,
  Let thy salvation visit me.

PSALM CVI.

5 O may I worthy prove to see
　Thy saints in full prosperity;
　That I the joyful choir may join,
　And count thy peoples' triumph mine.
6 But ah! can we expect such grace,
　Of parents vile the viler race;
　Who their misdeeds have acted o'er,
　And with new crimes increas'd the score?
7 Ingrateful, they no longer thought
　On all his works in Egypt wrought;
　The Red Sea they no sooner view'd
　Than they their base distrust renew'd.
8 Yet he, to vindicate his Name,
　Once more to their deliv'rance came;
　To make his sov'reign pow'r be known,
　That he is God, and he alone.
9 To right and left, at his command,
　The parting deep disclos'd her sand;
　Where firm and dry the passage lay,
　As through some parch'd and desert way.
10 Thus rescu'd from their foes they were,
　Who closely press'd upon their rear;
11 Whose rage pursu'd them to those waves,
　That prov'd the rash pursuers' graves.
12 The wat'ry mountains' sudden fall
　O'erwhelm'd proud Pharaoh, host and all;
　This proof did stupid Israel move
　To own God's truth, and praise his love.

PART II.

13 But soon these wonders they forgot,
　And for his counsel waited not;
14 But lusting in the wilderness,
　Did him with fresh temptations press.
15 Strong food at their request he sent,
　But made their sin their punishment;
16 Yet still his saints they did oppose,
　The priest and prophet whom he chose.
17 But earth, the quarrel to decide,
　Her vengeful jaws extending wide,
　Rash Dathan to her centre drew,
　With proud Abiram's factious crew.
18 The rest of those who did conspire
　To kindle wild sedition's fire,
　With all their impious train, became
　A prey to heav'n's devouring flame.
19 Near Horeb's mount a calf they made,
　And to the molten image pray'd;
20 Adoring what their hands did frame,
　They chang'd their glory to their shame.

21 Their God and Saviour they forgot,
   And all his works in Egypt wrought;
22 His signs in Ham's astonish'd coast,
   And where proud Pharaoh's troops were lost.
23 Thus urg'd, his vengeful hand he rear'd,
   But Moses in the breach appear'd;
   The saint did for the rebels pray,
   And turn'd heav'n's kindled wrath away.
24 Yet they his pleasant land despis'd,
   Nor his repeated promise priz'd,
25 Nor did th' Almighty's voice obey;
   But when God said, Go up, would stay.
26 This seal'd their doom, without redress
   To perish in the wilderness;
27 Or else to be by heathens' hands
   O'erthrown, and scatter'd through the lands.

PART III.

28 Yet, unreclaim'd, this stubborn race
   Baal-Peor's worship did embrace;
   Became his impious guests, and fed
   On sacrifices to the dead.
29 Thus they persisted to provoke
   God's vengeance to the final stroke:
   'Tis come—the deadly pest is come,
   To execute their gen'ral doom.
30 But Phineas, fir'd with holy rage,
   Th' Almighty vengeance to assuage,
   Did, by two bold offenders' fall,
   Th' atonement make that ransom'd all.
31 As him a heav'nly zeal had mov'd,
   So heav'n the zealous act approv'd;
   To him confirming, and his race,
   The priesthood he so well did grace.
32 At Meribah God's wrath they mov'd;
   Who Moses, for their sakes reprov'd;
33 Whose patient soul they did provoke,
   Till rashly the meek prophet spoke.
34 Nor, when possess'd of Canaan's land,
   Did they perform their Lord's command,
   Nor his commission'd sword employ
   The guilty nations to destroy.
35 Not only spar'd the pagan crew,
   But, mingling, learnt their vices too;
36 And worship to those idols paid,
   Which them to fatal snares betray'd.
37, 38 To devils they did sacrifice
   Their children, with relentless eyes;
   Approach'd their altars through a flood
   Of their own sons and daughters' blood.

No cheaper victims would appease
Canaan's remorseless deities;
No blood her idols reconcile,
But that which did the land defile.

PART IV.

39 Nor did these savage cruelties
The harden'd reprobate suffice;
For after their heart's lust they went,
And daily did new crimes invent.

40 But sins of such infernal hue
God's wrath against his people drew,
Till he, their once indulgent Lord,
His own inheritance abhor'd.

41 He them defenceless did expose,
To their insulting heathen foes;
And made them on the triumph wait
Of those who bore them greatest hate.

42 Nor thus his indignation ceas'd;
Their list of tyrants still increas'd,
Till they, who God's mild sway declin'd,
Were made the vassals of mankind.

43 Yet when, distress'd, they did repent,
His anger did as oft relent;
But freed, they did his wrath provoke,
Renew'd their sins, and he their yoke.

44 Nor yet implacable he prov'd,
Nor heard their wretched cries unmov'd;

45 But did to mind his promise bring,
And mercy's inexhausted spring.

46 Compassion too he did impart
Ev'n to their foes' obdurate heart;
And pity for their suff'rings bred
In those who them to bondage led.

47 Still save us, Lord, and Israel's bands,
Together bring from heathen lands;
So to thy Name our thanks we'll raise,
And ever triumph in thy praise.

48 Let Israel's God be ever bless'd,
His Name eternally confess'd:
Let all his saints, with full accord,
Sing loud Amens—Praise ye the Lord.

PSALM CVII.

1 TO God your grateful voices raise,
who does your daily Patron prove;
And let your never-ceasing praise
attend on his eternal love.

2, 3 Let those give thanks, whom he from bands
of proud oppressing foes releas'd;

And brought them back from diſtant lands,
  from north and ſouth, and weſt and eaſt.
4, 5 Through lonely deſert ways they went,
  nor could a peopled city find;
Till quite with thirſt and hunger ſpent,
  their fainting ſouls within them pin'd.
6 Then ſoon to God's indulgent ear
  did they their mournful cry addreſs;
Who graciouſly vouchſaf'd to hear,
  And freed them from their deep diſtreſs.
7 From crooked paths he led them forth,
  and in the certain way did guide
To wealthy towns, of great reſort,
  where all their wants were well ſupply'd.
8 O then that all the earth with me
  would God, for this his goodneſs, praiſe;
And for the mighty works which he
  throughout the wond'ring world diſplays!
9 For he from heav'n the ſad eſtate
  of longing ſouls with pity views;
To hungry ſouls, that pant for meat,
  his goodneſs daily food renews.

PART II.

10 Some lie, with darkneſs compaſs'd round,
  in death's uncomfortable ſhade,
And with unwieldy fetters bound,
  by preſſing cares more heavy made.
11, 12 Becauſe God's counſels they defy'd,
  and lightly priz'd his holy word,
With theſe afflictions they were try'd;
  they fell, and none could help afford.
13 Then ſoon to God's indulgent ear
  did they their mournful cry addreſs;
Who graciouſly vouchſaf'd to hear,
  and freed them from their deep diſtreſs.
14 From diſmal dungeons, dark as night,
  and ſhades, as black as death's abode,
He brought them forth to chearful light,
  and welcome liberty beſtow'd.
15 O then that all the earth with me
  would God, for this his goodneſs, praiſe;
And for the mighty works which he
  throughout the wond'ring world diſplays!
16 For he, with his Almighty hand,
  the gates of braſs in pieces broke;
Nor could the maſſy bars withſtand,
  or temper'd ſteel reſiſt his ſtroke.

PART

PSALM CVII.
PART III.

17 Remorseless wretches, void of sense,
  with bold transgressions God defy;
And, for their multiply'd offence,
  oppress'd with sore diseases lie.

18 Their soul, a prey to pain and fear,
  abhors to taste the choicest meats;
And they by faint degrees draw near
  to death's inhospitable gates.

19 Then straight to God's indulgent ear
  do they their mournful cry address;
Who graciously vouchsafes to hear,
  and frees them from their deep distress.

20 He all their sad distempers heals,
  his word both health and safety gives;
And, when all human succour fails,
  from near destruction them retrieves.

21 O then that all the earth with me
  would God, for this his goodness, praise;
And for the mighty works which he
  throughout the wond'ring world displays!

22 With off'rings let his altar flame,
  whilst they their grateful thanks express,
And with loud joy his holy Name,
  for all his acts of wonder, bless.

PART IV.

23, 24 They that in ships, with courage bold,
  o'er swelling waves their trade pursue,
Do God's amazing works behold,
  and in the deep his wonders view.

25 No sooner his command is past,
  than forth the dreadful tempest flies,
Which sweeps the sea with rapid haste,
  and makes the stormy billows rise.

26 Sometimes the ships, toss'd up to heav'n,
  on tops of mountain waves appear;
Then down the steep abyss are driv'n,
  whilst ev'ry soul dissolves with fear.

27 They reel and stagger to and fro,
  like men with fumes of wine oppress'd;
Nor do the skilful seamen know
  which way to steer, what course is best.

28 Then straight to God's indulgent ear
  they do their mournful cry address;
Who graciously vouchsafes to hear,
  and frees them from their deep distress.

29, 30 He does the raging storm appease,
  and makes the billows calm and still;

With joy they see their fury cease,
   and their intendid course fulfil.
31 O then that all the earth with me
   would God, for this his goodness, praise;
And for the mighty works which he
   throughout the wond'ring world displays!
32 Let them, where all the tribes resort,
   advance to heav'n his glorious Name,
And in the elder's sov'reign court,
   with one consent his praise proclaim.

PART V.

33, 34 A fruitful land, where streams abound,
   God's just revenge, if people sin,
Will turn to dry and barren ground,
   to punish those that dwell therein.
35, 36 The parch'd and desert heath he makes
   to flow with streams and springing wells,
Which for his lot the hungry takes,
   and in strong cities safely dwells.
37, 38 He sows the field, the vineyard plants,
   which gratefully his toil repay;
Nor can, whilst God his blessing grants,
   his fruitful seed or stock decay.
39 But when his sins heav'n's wrath provoke,
   his health and substance fade away;
He feels th' oppressor's galling yoke,
   and is of grief the wretched prey.
40 The prince that slights what God commands,
   expos'd to scorn, must quit his throne;
And over wild and desert lands,
   where no path offers, stray alone:
41 Whilst God, from all afflicting cares,
   sets up the humble man on high,
And makes in time his num'rous heirs
   with his increasing flocks to vie.
42, 43 Then sinners shall have nought to say,
   the just a decent joy shall show;
The wise these strange events shall weigh,
   and thence God's goodness fully know.

PSALM CVIII.

1 O God, my heart is fully bent
   to magnify thy Name;
My tongue with chearful songs of praise
   shall celebrate thy fame.
2 Awake, my lute; nor thou, my harp,
   thy warbling notes delay;
Whilst I with early hymns of joy
   prevent the dawning day.

PSALM CIX.

3 To all the lift'ning tribes, O Lord,
   thy wonders I will tell,
And to thofe nations fing thy praife,
   that round about us dwell;
4 Becaufe thy mercy's boundlefs height
   the higheft heav'n tranfcends,
And far beyond th' afpiring clouds
   thy faithful truth extends.
5 Be thou, O God, exalted high
   above the ftarry frame;
And let the world, with one confent,
   confefs thy glorious Name.
6 That all thy chofen people thee
   their Saviour may declare;
Let thy right-hand protect me ftill,
   and anfwer thou my pray'r.
7 Since God himfelf hath faid the word,
   whofe promife cannot fail,
With joy I Sechem will divide,
   and meafure Succoth's vale.
8 Gilead is mine, Manaffeh too,
   and Ephraim owns my caufe;
Their ftrength my regal pow'r fupports,
   and Judah gives my laws.
9 Moab I'll make my fervile drudge,
   on vanquifh'd Edom tread;
And through the proud Philiftine lands
   my conq'ring banners fpread.
10 By whofe fupport and aid fhall I
   their well-fenc'd city gain?
Who will my troops fecurely lead
   through Edom's guarded plain?
11 Lord, wilt not thou affift our arms,
   which late thou didft forfake?
And wilt not thou of thefe our hofts
   once more the guidance take?
12 O to thy fervant in diftrefs
   thy fpeedy fuccour fend;
For vain it is on human aid
   for fafety to depend.
13 Then valiant acts fhall we perform,
   if thou thy pow'r difclofe;
For God it is, and God alone,
   that treads down all our foes.

PSALM CIX.

1 O God, whofe former mercies make
   my conftant praife thy due,
Hold not thy peace, but my fad ftate
   with wonted favour view:

2 For sinful men, with lying lips,
    deceitful speeches frame,
  And with their study'd slanders seek
    to wound my spotless fame.
3 Their restless hatred prompts them still
    malicious lies to spread;
  And all against my life combine,
    by causeless fury led.
4 Those whom with tend'rest love I us'd,
    my chief opposers are;
  Whilst I, of other friends bereft,
    resort to thee by pray'r.
5 Since mischief, for the good I did,
    their strange reward does prove,
  And hatred's the return they make
    for undissembled love.
6 Their guilty leaders shall be made
    to some ill man a slave;
  And, when he's try'd, his mortal foe
    for his accuser have.
7 His guilt, when sentence is pronounc'd,
    shall meet a dreadful fate,
  Whilst his rejected pray'r but serves
    his crimes to aggravate.
8 He, snatch'd by some untimely fate,
    sha'n't live out half his days;
  Another, by divine decree,
    shall on his office seize.
9, 10 His seed shall orphans be, his wife
    a widow plung'd in grief;
  His vagrant children beg their bread,
    where none can give relief.
11 His ill-got riches shall be made
    to usurers a prey;
  The fruit of all his toil shall be
    by strangers borne away.
12 None shall be found that to his wants
    their mercy will extend,
  Or to his helpless orphan seed
    the least assistance lend.
13 A swift destruction soon shall seize
    on his unhappy race;
  And the next age his hated name
    shall utterly deface.
14 The vengeance of his father's sins
    upon his head shall fall;
  God on his mothers crimes shall think,
    and punish him for all.

PSALM CIX.

15 All these, in horrid order rank'd,
   before the Lord shall stand,
Till his fierce anger quite cuts off
   their mem'ry from the land.

PART II.

16 Because he never mercy show'd,
   but still the poor opprefs'd;
And sought to slay the helpless man,
   with heavy woes distress'd.
17 Therefore the curse he lov'd to vent
   shall his own portion prove;
And blessing which he still abhorr'd,
   shall far from him remove.
18 Since he in cursing took such pride,
   like water it shall spread,
Through all his veins, and stick like oil,
   with which his bones are fed.
19 This, like a poison'd robe, shall still
   his constant cov'ring be,
Or an envenom'd belt, from which
   he never shall be free.
20 Thus shall the Lord reward all those
   that ill to me design;
That with malicous false reports
   against my life combine.
21 But for thy glorious Name, O God,
   do thou deliver me;
And for thy plenteous mercy's sake,
   preserve and set me free.
22 For I, to utmost straits reduc'd,
   am void of all relief;
My heart is wounded with distress,
   and quite pierc'd through with grief.
23 I, like an ev'ning shade, decline,
   which vanishes apace;
Like locusts, up and down I'm tofs'd,
   and have no certain place.
24, 25 My knees with fasting are grown weak,
   my body lank and lean;
All that behold me shake their heads,
   and treat me with disdain.
26, 27 But for thy mercy's sake, O Lord,
   do thou my foes withstand;
That all may see 'tis thy own act,
   the work of thy right-hand.
28 Then let them curse, so thou but bless;
   let shame the portion be
Of all that my destruction seek,
   while I rejoice in thee.

29 My foe shall with disgrace be cloath'd;
 and, spite of all his pride,
His own confusion, like a cloak,
 the guilty wretch shall hide.
30 But I to God, in grateful thanks,
 my chearful voice will raise;
And where the great assembly meets,
 set forth his noble praise.
31 For him the poor shall always find
 their sure and constant friend;
And he shall from unrighteous dooms
 their guiltless souls defend.

PSALM CX.

1 THE Lord unto my Lord thus spake,
 "Till I thy foes thy footstool make,
2 " sit thou, in state, at my right-hand:
" Supreme in Sion thou shalt be,
" And all thy proud opposers see
 " subjected to thy just command.
3 " Thee, in thy pow'r's triumphant day,
" The willing nations shall obey:
 " and, when thy rising beams they view,
" Shall all, redeem'd from error's night,
" Appear as numberless and bright
 " as crystal drops of morning dew."
4 The Lord hath sworn, nor sworn in vain,
That, like Melchisedech's, thy reign
 and priesthood shall no period know:
5 No proud competitor to sit
At thy right-hand will he permit,
 but in his wrath crown'd heads o'erthrow.
6 The sentenc'd heathen he shall slay,
And fill with carcases his way,
 till he hath struck earth's tyrants dead;
7 But in the high-way brooks shall first,
Like a poor pilgrim, slake his thirst,
 and then in triumph raise his head.

PSALM CXI.

1 PRaise ye the Lord; our God to praise
 My soul her utmost pow'rs shall raise;
With private friends, and in the throng
Of saints, his praise shall be my song.
2 His works, for greatness though renown'd,
His wond'rous works with ease are found
By those who seek for them aright,
And in the pious search delight.
3 His works are all of matchless fame,
And universal glory claim;

PSALM CXII.

 His truth, confirm'd through ages paft,
 Shall to eternal ages laft.
4 By precepts he hath us enjoin'd,
 To keep his wond'rous works in mind;
 And to pofterity record,
 That good and gracious is our Lord.
5 His bounty, like a flowing tide,
 Has all his fervants' wants fupply'd;
 And he will ever keep in mind
 His cov'nant with our fathers fign'd.
6 At once aftonifh'd and o'erjoy'd,
 They faw his matchlefs pow'r employ'd,
 Whereby the heathen were fupprefs'd,
 And we their heritage poffefs'd.
7 Juft are the dealings of his hands,
 Immutable are his commands,
8 By truth and equity fuftain'd,
 And for eternal rules ordain'd.
9 He fet his faints from bondage free,
 And then eftablifh'd his decree,
 For ever to remain the fame:
 Holy and rev'rend is his Name.
10 Who wifdom's facred prize would win,
 Muft with the fear of God begin:
 Immortal praife and heav'nly fkill
 Have they who know and do his will.

PSALM CXII.

HALLELUJAH.

1 THAT man is bleft who ftands in awe
 Of God, and loves his facred law;
2 His feed on earth fhall be renown'd,
 And with fucceffive honours crown'd.
3 His houfe, the feat of wealth, fhall be
 An inexhaufted treafury;
 His juftice, free from all decay,
 Shall bleffings to his heirs convey.
4 The foul that's fill'd with virtue's light
 Shines brighteft in affliction's night;
 To pity the diftrefs'd inclin'd,
 As well as juft to all mankind.
5 His lib'ral favours he extends,
 To fome he gives, to others lends;
 Yet what his charity impairs,
 He faves by prudence in affairs.
6 Befet with threat'ning dangers round,
 Unmov'd fhall he maintain his ground:
 The fweet remembrance of the juft
 Shall flourifh when he fleeps in duft.

7 Ill tidings never can surprise
　His heart, that, fix'd, on God relies:
8 On safety's rock he sits and sees
　The shipwreck of his enemies.
9 His hands, while they his alms bestow'd,
　His glory's future harvest sow'd,
　Whence he shall reap wealth, fame, renown,
　A temp'ral and eternal crown.
10 The wicked shall his triumph see,
　And gnash their teeth in agony;
　While their unrighteous hopes decay,
　And vanish with themselves away.

PSALM CXIII.

1 YE saints and servants of the Lord,
　　The triumphs of his Name record;
2 　his sacred Name for ever bless:
3 Where'er the circling sun displays
　His rising beams or setting rays,
　　due praise to his great Name address.
4 God through the world extends his sway:
　The regions of eternal day
　　but shadows of his glory are:
5 With him whose majesty excels,
　Who made the heav'n in which he dwells,
　　let no created pow'r compare.
6 Though 'tis beneath his state to view
　In highest heav'n what angels do,
　　yet he to earth vouchsafes his care:
　He takes the needy from his cell,
　Advancing him in courts to dwell,
　　companion to the greatest there.
7 When childless families despair,
　He sends the blessing of an heir,
　　to rescue their expiring name;
　Makes her that barren was to bear,
　And joyfully her fruit to rear:
　　O then extol his matchless fame!

PSALM CXIV.

1 WHEN Israel by th' Almighty led,
　　enrich'd with their oppressors' spoil,
　From Egypt march'd, and Jacob's seed
　　from bondage in a foreign soil;
2 Jehovah, for his residence,
　　chose out imperial Judah's tent,
　His mansion royal, and from thence
　　through Israel's camp his orders sent.
3 The distant sea with terror saw,
　　and from the Almighty's presence fled;

Old

PSALM CXV.

    Old Jordan's streams, surpris'd with awe,
      retreated to their fountain's head.
4 The taller mountains skipp'd like rams,
      when danger near the fold they hear;
    The hills skipp'd after them like lambs
      affrighted by their leader's fear.
5 O sea! what made your tide withdraw,
      and naked leave your oozy bed?
    Why, Jordan, against nature's law,
      recoild'st thou to thy fountain's head?
6 Why, mountains, did ye skip like rams,
      when danger does approach the fold?
    Why after you the hills, like lambs
      when they their leader's flight behold?
7 Earth, tremble on; well may'st thou fear
      thy Lord and Maker's face to see;
    When Jacob's awful God draws near,
      'tis time for earth and seas to flee.
8 To flee from God, who nature's law
      confirms and cancels at his will;
    Who springs from flinty rocks can draw,
      and thirsty vales with water fill.

PSALM CXV.

1 LORD, not to us, we claim no share,
      but to thy sacred Name
    Give glory, for thy mercy's sake,
      and truth's eternal fame.
2 Why should the heathen cry, Where's now
      the God whom we adore?
3 Convince them that in heav'n thou art,
      and uncontroul'd thy pow'r.
4 Their gods but gold and silver are,
      the works of mortal hands;
5 With speechless mouth and sightless eyes
      the molten idol stands.
6 The pageant has both ears and nose,
      but neither hears nor smells;
7 Its hands and feet nor feel nor move;
      no life within it dwells.
8 Such senseless stocks they are, that we
      can nothing like them find,
    But those who on their help rely,
      and them for gods design'd.
9 O Israel, make the Lord your trust,
      who is your help and shield;
10 Priests, Levites, trust in him alone,
      who only help can yield.

11 Let all who truly fear the Lord,
   on him they fear rely;
Who them in danger can defend,
   and all their wants supply.
12, 13 Of us he oft has mindful been,
   and Israel's house will bless;
Priests, Levites, proselytes, ev'n all
   who his great Name confess.
14 On you, and on your heirs, he will
   increase of blessings bring;
15 Thrice happy you, who fav'rites are
   of this Almighty King!
16 Heav'n's highest orb of glory he
   his empire's seat design'd;
And gave this lower globe of earth
   a portion to mankind.
17 They who in death and silence sleep,
   to him no praise afford;
18 But we will bless for evermore
   our ever-living Lord.

PSALM CXVI.

1 MY soul with grateful thoughts of love
      entirely is possest,
Because the Lord vouchsaf'd to hear
   the voice of my request.
2 Since he has now his ear inclin'd,
   I never will despair;
But still in all the straits of life
   to him address my pray'r.
3 With deadly sorrows compass'd round,
   with pains of hell oppress'd;
When trouble seiz'd my aching heart,
   and anguish rack'd my breast;
4 On God's Almighty Name I call'd,
   and thus to him I pray'd,
   "Lord, I beseech thee, save my soul,
   "with sorrow quite dismay'd."
5, 6 How just and merciful is God!
   how gracious is the Lord!
Who saves the harmless, and to me
   does timely help afford.
7 Then, free from pensive cares, my soul,
   resume thy wonted rest;
For God has wond'rously to thee
   his bounteous love exprest.
8 When death alarm'd me, he remov'd
   my dangers and my fears;
My feet from falling he secur'd,
   and dry'd my eyes from tears.

9 Therefore

9 Therefore my life's remaining years,
   which God to me shall lend,
Will I in praises to his Name,
   and in his service spend.
10, 11 In God I trusted, and of him
   in greatest straits did boast;
For in my flight all hopes of aid
   from faithless men were lost.
12, 13 Then what return to him shall I
   for all his goodness make?
I'll praise his Name, and with glad zeal
   the cup of blessing take.
14, 15 I'll pay my vows among his saints,
   whose blood, howe'er despis'd
By wicked men, in God's account
   is always highly priz'd.
16 By various ties, O Lord, must I
   to thy dominion bow;
Thy humble handmaid's son before,
   thy ransom'd captive now!
17, 18 To thee I'll off'rings bring of praise;
   and, whilst I bless thy Name,
The just performance of my vows
   to all thy saints proclaim.
19 They in Jerusalem shall meet,
   and in thy house shall join,
To bless thy Name with one consent,
   and mix their songs with mine.

PSALM CXVII.

1 WITH chearful notes let all the earth
      to heav'n their voices raise;
Let all, inspir'd with godly mirth,
   sing solemn hymns of praise.
2 God's tender mercy knows no bound,
   his truth shall ne'er decay;
Then let the willing nations round
   their grateful tribute pay.

PSALM CXVIII.

1, 2 O Praise the Lord, for he is good,
      his mercies ne'er decay;
That his kind favours ever last,
   let thankful Israel say.
3, 4 Their sense of his eternal love
   let Aaron's house express;
And that it never fails, let all
   that fear the Lord confess.
5 To God I made my humble moan,
   with troubles quite opprest;

K 2   And

PSALM CXVIII.

And he releas'd me from my straits,
  and granted my request.
6 Since therefore God does on my side
  so graciously appear,
Why should the vain attempts of men
  possess my soul with fear?
7 Since God with those that aid my cause
  vouchsafes my part to take,
To all my foes I need not doubt
  a just return to make.

8, 9 For better 'tis to trust in God,
  and have the Lord our friend,
Than on the greatest human pow'r,
  for safety to depend.
10, 11 Though many nations, closely leagu'd,
  did oft beset me round;
Yet, by his boundless pow'r sustain'd
  I did their strength confound.

12 They swarm'd like bees, and yet their rage
  was but a short-liv'd blaze;
For whilst on God I still rely'd,
  I vanquish'd them with ease.
13 When all united press'd me hard,
  in hopes to make me fall,
The Lord vouchsaf'd to take my part,
  and save me from them all.

14 The honour of my strange escape
  to him alone belongs;
He is my Saviour and my strength,
  he only claims my songs.
15 Joy fills the dwelling of the just,
  whom God has sav'd from harm;
For wond'rous things are brought to pass
  by his Almighty arm.

16 He, by his own resistless pow'r,
  has endless honour won;
The saving strength of his right-hand
  amazing works has done.
17 God will not suffer me to fall,
  but still prolongs my days;
That, by declaring all his works,
  I may advance his praise.
18 When God had sorely me chastis'd
  till quite of hopes bereav'd,
His mercy from the gates of death
  my fainting life repriev'd.
19 Then open wide the temple gates,
  to which the just repair,

That

PSALM CXIX.

That I may enter in and praise
   my great Deliv'rer there.
20, 21 Within those gates of God's abode,
   to which the righteous press,
Since thou hast heard, and set me safe,
   thy holy Name I'll bless.
22, 23 That which the builders once refus'd,
   is now the corner stone ;
This is the wond'rous work of God,
   the work of God alone.
24, 25 This day is God's ; let all the land
   exalt their chearful voice ;
Lord, we beseech thee, save us now,
   and make us still rejoice.
26 Him that approaches in God's Name
   let all the assembly bless ;
" We that belong to God's own house
" have wish'd you good success."
27 God is the Lord, through whom we all
   both light and comfort find ;
Fast to the altar's horn, with cords,
   the chosen victim bind.
28 Thou art my Lord, O God, and still
   I'll praise thy holy Name ;
Because thou only art my God,
   I'll celebrate thy fame.
29 O then with me give thanks to God,
   who still does gracious prove ;
And let the tribute of our praise
   be endless as his love.

PSALM CXIX.
ALEPH.

1 HOW bless'd are they, who always keep
   the pure and perfect way !
Who never from the sacred paths
   of God's commandments stray !
2 How bless'd, who to his righteous laws
   have still obedient been !
And have with fervent humble zeal
   his favour sought to win !
3 Such men their utmost caution use
   to shun each wicked deed ;
But in the path which he directs
   with constant care proceed.
4 Thou strictly hast enjoin'd us, Lord,
   to learn thy sacred will ;
And all our diligence employ
   thy statutes to fulfil.

5 O then that thy most holy will
   might o'er my ways preside,
 And I the course of all my life
   by thy direction guide!
6 Then with assurance should I walk,
   from all confusion free;
 Convinc'd, with joy, that all my ways
   with thy commands agree.
7 My upright heart shall my glad mouth
   with chearful praises fill;
 When, by thy righteous judgments taught,
   I shall have learnt thy will.
8 So to thy sacred laws shall I
   all due observance pay;
 O then forsake me not, my God,
   nor cast me quite away.

BETH.

9 How shall the young preserve their ways
   from all pollution free?
 By making still their course of life
   with thy commands agree.
10 With hearty zeal for thee I seek,
   to thee for succour pray;
 O suffer not my careless steps
   from thy right paths to stray.
11 Safe in my heart, and closely hid,
   thy word, my treasure, lies;
 To succour me with timely aid,
   when sinful thoughts arise.
12 Secur'd by that, my grateful soul
   shall ever bless thy Name;
 O teach me then by thy just laws
   my future life to frame.
13 My lips, unlock'd by pious zeal,
   to others have declar'd
 How well the judgments of thy mouth
   deserve our best regard.
14 Whilst in the way of thy commands
   more solid joy I found,
 Than had I been with vast increase
   of envy'd riches crown'd.
15 Therefore thy just and upright laws,
   shall always fill my mind;
 And those sound rules which thou prescrib'st,
   all due respect shall find.
16 To keep thy statutes undefac'd
   shall be my constant joy;
 The strict remembrance of thy word
   shall all my thoughts employ.

GIMEL.

PSALM CXIX.

GIMEL.

17 Be gracious to thy servant, Lord,
  do thou my life defend,
 That I, according to thy word,
  my future time may spend.
18 Enlighten both my eyes and mind,
  that so I may discern
 The wond'rous works which they behold,
  who thy just precepts learn.
19 Though, like a stranger in the land,
  from place to place I stray,
 Thy righteous judgments from my sight
  remove not thou away.
20 My fainting soul is almost pin'd,
  with earnest longing spent,
 Whilst always on the eager search
  of thy just will intent.
21 Thy sharp rebuke shall crush the proud,
  whom still thy curse pursues;
 Since they to walk in thy right ways
  presumptuously refuse.
22 But far from me do thou, O Lord,
  contempt and shame remove;
 For I thy sacred laws affect
  with undissembled love.
23 Though princes oft, in council met,
  against thy servant spake;
 Yet I thy statutes to observe
  my constant bus'ness make.
24 For thy commands have always been
  my comfort and delight;
 By them I learn, with prudent care
  to guide my steps aright.

DALETH.

25 My soul, oppress'd with deadly care,
  close to the dust does cleave;
 Revive me, Lord, and let me now
  thy promis'd aid receive.
26 To thee I still declar'd my ways,
  and thou inclind'st thine ear;
 O teach me then my future life
  by thy just laws to steer.
27 If thou wilt make me know thy laws,
  and by their guidance walk,
 The wond'rous works which thou hast done
  shall be my constant talk.
28 But see, my soul within me sinks,
  press'd down with weighty care;

Do thou, according to thy word,
my wasted strength repair.
29 Far, far from me be all false ways
and lying arts remov'd;
But kindly grant I still may keep
the path by thee approv'd.
30 Thy faithful ways, thou God of truth,
my happy choice I've made;
Thy judgments, as my rule of life,
before me always laid.
31 My care has been to make my life
with thy commands agree;
O then preserve thy servant, Lord,
from shame and ruin free.
32 So in the way of thy commands
shall I with pleasure run,
And, with a heart enlarg'd with joy,
successfully go on.

H E.

33 Instruct me in thy statutes, Lord,
thy righteous paths display;
And I from them, through all my life,
will never go astray.
34 If thou true wisdom from above
wilt graciously impart,
To keep thy perfect laws I will
devote my zealous heart.
35 Direct me in the sacred ways
to which thy precepts lead;
Because my chief delight has been
thy righteous paths to tread.
36 Do thou to thy most just commands
incline my willing heart;
Let no desire of worldly wealth
from thee my thoughts divert.
37 From those vain objects turn my eyes,
which this false world displays;
But give me lively pow'r and strength
to keep thy righteous ways.
38 Confirm the promise which thou mad'st,
and give thy servant aid,
Who to transgress thy sacred laws
is awfully afraid.
39 The foul disgrace I justly fear,
in mercy, Lord, remove;
For all the judgments thou ordain'st
are full of grace and love.
40 Thou know'st how after thy commands,
my longing heart does pant;

O then

PSALM CXIX.

O then make haste to raise me up,
 and promis'd succour grant.

VAU.

41 Thy constant blessing, Lord, bestow,
 to cheer my drooping heart;
 To me, according to thy word,
 thy saving health impart.
42 So shall I, when my foes upbraid,
 this ready answer make;
 " In God I trust, who never will
 " his faithful promise break."
43 Then let not quite the word of truth
 be from my mouth remov'd;
 Since still my ground of stedfast hope
 thy just decrees have prov'd.
44 So I to keep thy righteous laws
 will all my study bend;
 From age to age my time to come
 in their observance spend.
45 E'er long I trust to walk at large,
 from all incumbrance free;
 Since I resolve to make my life
 with thy commands agree.
46 Thy laws shall be my constant talk;
 and princes shall attend,
 Whilst I the justice of thy ways
 with confidence defend.
47 My longing heart and ravish'd soul
 shall both o'erflow with joy,
 When in thy lov'd commandments I
 my happy hours employ.
48 Then will I to thy just decrees
 lift up my willing hands;
 My care and bus'ness then shall be
 to study thy commands.

ZAIN.

49 According to thy promis'd grace,
 thy favour, Lord, extend;
 Make good to me the word on which
 thy servant's hopes depend.
50 That only comfort in distress
 did all my griefs controul;
 Thy word, when troubles hemm'd me round,
 reviv'd my fainting soul.
51 Insulting foes did proudly mock,
 and all my hopes deride;
 Yet from thy law not all their scoffs
 could make me turn aside.

52 Thy judgments then, of ancient date,
 I quickly call'd to mind,
Till, ravish'd with such thoughts, my soul
 did speedy comfort find.
53 Sometimes I stand amaz'd, like one
 with deadly horror struck,
To think how all my sinful foes
 have thy just laws forsook.
54 But I thy statutes and decrees
 my chearful anthems made:
Whilst through strange lands and desert wilds
 I like a pilgrim stray'd.
55 Thy Name, that cheer'd my heart by day,
 has fill'd my thoughts by night:
I then resolv'd by thy just laws
 to guide my steps aright.
56 That peace of mind, which has my soul
 in deep distress sustain'd,
By strict obedience to thy will
 I happily obtain'd.

CHETH.

57 O Lord, my God, my portion thou
 and sure possession art;
Thy words I stedfastly resolve
 to treasure in my heart.
58 With all the strength of warm desire
 I did thy grace implore;
Disclose, according to thy word,
 thy mercy's boundless store.
59 With due reflection and strict care
 on all my ways I thought;
And so, reclaim'd to thy just paths,
 my wand'ring steps I brought.
60 'I lost no time, but made great haste,
 resolv'd, without delay,
To watch, that I might never more
 from thy commandments stray.
61 Though num'rous troops of sinful men
 to rob me have combin'd,
Yet I thy pure and righteous laws
 have ever kept in mind.
62 In dead of night I will arise
 to sing thy solemn praise;
Convinc'd how much I always ought
 to love thy righteous ways.
63 To such as fear thy holy Name
 myself I closely join;
To all who their obedient wills
 to thy commands resign.

64 O'er

64 O'er all the earth thy mercy, Lord,
    abundantly is shed;
  O make me then exactly learn
    thy sacred paths to tread.

TETH.

65 With me, thy servant, thou hast dealt
    most graciously, O Lord;
  Repeated benefits bestow'd,
    according to thy word.

66 Teach me the sacred skill, by which
    right judgment is attain'd,
  Who in belief of thy commands
    have steadfastly remain'd.

67 Before affliction stopp'd my course,
    my foot-steps went astray;
  But I have since been disciplin'd
    thy precepts to obey.

68 Thou art, O Lord, supremely good,
    and all thou dost is so;
  On me, thy statutes to discern,
    thy saving skill bestow.

69 The proud have forg'd malicious lies,
    my spotless fame to stain;
  But my fix'd heart, without reserve,
    thy precepts shall retain.

70 While pamper'd, they, with prosp'rous ills,
    in sensual pleasures live,
  My soul can relish no delight,
    but what thy precepts give.

71 'Tis good for me that I have felt
    affliction's chast'ning rod,
  That I might duly learn and keep
    the statutes of my God.

72 The law that from thy mouth proceeds,
    of more esteem I hold
  Than untouch'd mines, than thousand mines
    of silver and of gold.

JOD.

73 To me, who am the workmanship
    of thy Almighty hands,
  The heav'nly understanding give
    to learn thy just commands.

74 My preservation to thy saints
    strong comfort will afford,
  To see success attend my hopes,
    who trusted in thy word.

75 That right thy judgments are, I now
    by sure experience see;

And that in faithfulness, O Lord,
   thou hast afflicted me..
76 O let thy tender mercy now
   afford me needful aid;
According to thy promise, Lord,
   to me, thy servant, made.
77 To me thy saving grace restore,
   that I again may live;
Whose soul can relish no delight,
   but what thy precepts give.
78 Defeat the proud, who, unprovok'd,
   to ruin me have sought,
Who only on thy sacred laws
   employ my harmless thought.
79 Let those that fear thy Name espouse
   my cause, and those alone,
Who have by strict and pious search,
   thy sacred precepts known.
80 In thy blest statutes let my heart
   continue always found;
That guilt and shame, the sinner's lot,
   may never me confound.

CAPH.

81 My soul with long expectance faints
   to see thy saving grace;
Yet still on thy unerring word
   my confidence I place.
82 My very eyes consume and fail
   with waiting for thy word;
O! when wilt thou thy kind relief
   and promis'd aid afford?
83 My skin like shrivel'd parchment shows,
   that long in smoke is set;
Yet no affliction me can force
   thy statutes to forget.
84 How many days must I endure
   of sorrow and distress?
When wilt thou judgment execute
   on them who me oppress?
85 The proud have digg'd a pit for me,
   that have no other foes,
But such as are averse to thee,
   and thy just laws oppose.
86 With sacred truth's eternal laws
   all thy commands agree;
Men persecute me without cause;
   thou, Lord, my helper be.
87 With close designs against my life
   they had almost prevail'd;

> But, in obedience to thy will,
> my duty never fail'd.

88 Thy wonted kindness, Lord, restore,
my drooping heart to cheer;
That by thy righteous statutes I
my life's whole course may steer.

LAMED.

89 For ever and for ever, Lord,
unchang'd thou dost remain;
Thy word, establish'd in the heav'ns,
does all their orbs sustain.

90 Through circling ages, Lord, thy truth
immoveable shall stand,
As doth the earth, which thou uphold'st
by thy Almighty hand.

91 All things the course by thee ordain'd
ev'n to this day fulfil;
They are thy faithful subjects all,
and servants of thy will.

92 Unless thy sacred law had been
my comfort and delight,
I must have fainted, and expir'd
in dark affliction's night.

93 Thy precepts therefore from my thoughts
shall never, Lord, depart;
For thou by them hast to new life
restor'd my dying heart.

94 As I am thine, entirely thine,
protect me, Lord, from harm,
Who have thy precepts sought to know,
and carefully perform.

95 The wicked have their ambush laid
my guiltless life to take;
But in the midst of danger I
thy word my study make.

96 I've seen an end of what we call
perfection here below;
But thy commandments, like thyself,
no change or period know.

MEM.

97 The love that to thy laws I bear
no language can display;
They with fresh wonders entertain
my ravish'd thoughts all day.

98 Through thy commands I wiser grow
than all my subtile foes;
For thy sure word doth me direct,
and all my ways dispose.

99 From me my former teachers now
    may abler counsel take;
Because thy sacred precepts I
    my constant study make.
100 In understanding I excel
    the sages of our days;
Because by thy unerring rules,
    I order all my ways.
101 My feet with care I have refrain'd,
    from ev'ry sinful way,
That to thy sacred word I might
    entire obedience pay.
102 I have not from thy judgments stray'd,
    by vain desires misled;
For, Lord, thou hast instructed me
    thy righteous paths to tread.
103 How sweet are all thy words to me!
    O what divine repast!
How much more grateful to my soul,
    than honey to my taste!
104 Taught by thy sacred precepts, I
    with heav'nly skill am blest,
Through which the treach'rous ways of sin
    I utterly detest.

N U N.

105 Thy word is to my feet a lamp,
    the way of truth to show;
A watch-light, to point out the path
    in which I ought to go.
106 I sware, and from my solemn oath
    will never start aside,
That in thy righteous judgments I
    will stedfastly abide.
107 Since I with griefs am so opprest,
    that I can bear no more,
According to thy word do thou
    my fainting soul restore.
108 Let still my sacrifice of praise
    with thee acceptance find;
And in thy righteous judgments, Lord,
    instruct my willing mind.
109 Though ghastly dangers me surround,
    my soul they cannot awe,
Nor with continual terrors keep
    from thinking on thy law.
110 My wicked and invet'rate foes
    for me their snares have laid;
Yet I have kept the upright path,
    nor from thy precepts stray'd.

111 Thy testimonies I have made
    my heritage and choice;
For they, when other comforts fail,
    my drooping heart rejoice.
112 My heart with early zeal began
    thy statutes to obey,
And till my course of life is done,
    shall keep thy upright way.

SAMECH.

113 Deceitful thoughts and practices
    I utterly detest;
But to thy law affection bear
    too great to be exprest.
114 My hiding-place, my refuge-tow'r,
    and shield art thou, O Lord;
I firmly anchor all my hopes
    on thy unerring word.
115 Hence, ye that trade in wickedness,
    approach not my abode;
For firmly I resolve to keep
    the precepts of my God.
116 According to thy gracious word,
    from danger set me free;
Nor make me of those hopes asham'd,
    that I repose in thee.
117 Uphold me, so shall I be safe,
    and rescu'd from distress;
To thy decrees continually
    my just respect address.
118 The wicked thou hast trod to earth,
    who from thy statutes stray'd;
Their vile deceit the just reward
    of their own falshood made.
119 The wicked from thy holy land
    thou dost like dross remove;
I therefore with such justice charm'd,
    thy testimonies love.
120 Yet with that love they make me dread,
    lest I should so offend,
When on transgressors I behold
    thy judgments thus descend.

AIN.

121 Judgment and justice I have lov'd;
    O therefore, Lord, engage
In my defence, nor give me up
    to my oppressors' rage.
122 Do thou be surety, Lord, for me,
    and so shall this distress

  Prove good for me; nor shall the proud
   my guiltless soul oppress.
123 My eyes, alas! begin to fail,
   in long expectance held;
  Till thy salvation they behold,
   and righteous word fulfill'd.
124 To me, thy servant, in distress,
   thy wonted grace display,
  And discipline my willing heart
   thy statutes to obey.
125 On me, devoted to thy fear,
   thy sacred skill bestow,
  That of thy testimonies I
   the full extent may know.
126 'Tis time, high time for thee, O Lord,
   thy vengeance to employ;
  When men with open violence
   thy sacred law destroy.
127 Yet their contempt of thy commands,
   but makes their value rise
  In my esteem, who purest gold,
   compar'd with them, despise.
128 Thy precepts therefore I account,
   in all respects, divine;
  They teach me to discern the right,
   and all false ways decline.

     P. E.

129 The wonders which thy laws contain
   no words can represent;
  Therefore to learn and practise them
   my zealous heart is bent.
130 The very entrance to thy word
   celestial light displays,
  And knowledge of true happiness
   to simplest minds conveys.
131 With eager hopes I waiting stood,
   and fainting with desire;
  That of thy wise commands I might
   the sacred skill acquire.
132 With favour, Lord, look down on me,
   who thy relief implore;
  As thou art wont to visit those
   who thy blest Name adore.
133 Directed by thy heav'nly word
   let all my foot-steps be;
  Nor wickedness of any kind
   dominion have o'er me.
134 Release, entirely set me free
   from persecuting hands,

PSALM CXIX.

That, unmolested, I may learn
and practise thy commands.
135 On me, devoted to thy fear,
Lord, make thy face to shine;
Thy statutes both to know and keep,
my heart with zeal incline.
136 My eyes to weeping fountains turn,
whence briny rivers flow,
To see mankind against thy laws
in bold defiance go.

TSADDI.

137 Thou art the righteous Judge, in whom
wrong'd innocence may trust:
And, like thyself, thy judgments, Lord,
in all respects are just.
138 Most just and true those statutes were,
which thou didst first decree;
And all with faithfulness perform'd
succeeding times shall see.
139 With zeal my flesh consumes away,
my soul with anguish frets,
To see my foes contemn at once
thy promises and threats.
140 Yet each neglected word of thine,
howe'er by them despis'd,
Is pure, and for eternal truth
by me, thy servant, priz'd.
141 Brought, for thy sake, to low estate,
contempt from all I find;
Yet no affronts or wrongs can drive
thy precepts from my mind.
142 Thy righteousness shall then endure,
when time itself is past;
Thy law is truth itself, that truth,
which shall for ever last.
143 Though trouble, anguish, doubts, and dread,
to compass me unite;
Beset with danger, still I make
thy precepts my delight.
144 Eternal and unerring rules
thy testimones give:
Teach me the wisdom that will make
my soul for ever live.

KOPH.

145 With my whole heart to God I call'd,
Lord, hear my earnest cry;
And I thy statutes to perform
will all my care apply.

146 Again

146 Again more fervently I pray'd,
    O save me, that I may
  Thy testimonies throughly know,
    and stedfastly obey.
147 My earlier pray'r the dawning day
    prevented, while I cry'd
  To him, on whose engaging word
    my hope alone rely'd.
148 With zeal have I awak'd before
    the midnight watch was set,
  That I of thy mysterious word
    might perfect knowledge get.
149 Lord, hear my supplicating voice,
    and wonted favour show:
  O quicken me, and so approve
    thy judgment ever true.
150 My persecuting foes advance,
    and hourly nearer draw;
  What treatment can I hope from them,
    who violate thy law?
151 Though they draw nigh, my comfort is,
    thou, Lord, art yet more near;
  Thou, whose commands are righteous all,
    thy promises sincere.
152 Concerning thy divine decrees,
    my soul has known of old,
  That they were true, and shall their truth
    to endless ages hold.

RESCH.

153 Consider my affliction, Lord,
    and me from bondage draw;
  Think on thy servant in distress,
    who ne'er forgets thy law.
154 Plead thou my cause; to that and me
    thy timely aid afford;
  With beams of mercy quicken me,
    according to thy word.
155 From harden'd sinners thou remov'st
    salvation far away;
  'Tis just thou should'st withdraw from them,
    who from thy statutes stray.
156 Since great thy tender mercies are
    to all who thee adore;
  According to thy judgments, Lord,
    my fainting hopes restore.
157 A num'rous host of spiteful foes
    against my life combine;
  But all too few to force my soul
    thy statutes to decline.

158 Those bold transgressors I beheld,
   and was with grief oppress'd,
   To see with what audacious pride
   thy cov'nant they transgress'd.
159 Yet while they slight, consider, Lord,
   how I thy precepts love;
   O therefore quicken me with beams
   of mercy from above.
160 As from the birth of time thy truth
   has held through ages past,
   So shall thy righteous judgments, firm,
   to endless ages last.

SCHIN.

161 Though mighty tyrants, without cause,
   conspire my blood to shed,
   Thy sacred word has pow'r alone
   to fill my heart with dread.
162 And yet that word my joyful breast
   with heav'nly rapture warms;
   Nor conquest, nor the spoils of war,
   have such transporting charms.
163 Perfidious practices and lies
   I utterly detest;
   But to thy laws affection bear,
   too vast to be exprest.
164 Sev'n times a day, with grateful voice,
   thy praises I resound,
   Because I find thy judgments all
   with truth and justice crown'd.
165 Secure, substantial peace have they
   who truly love thy law;
   No smiling mischief them can tempt,
   nor frowning danger awe.
166 For thy salvation I have hop'd,
   and though so long delay'd,
   With chearful zeal and strictest care
   all thy commands obey'd.
167 Thy testimonies I have kept,
   and constantly obey'd;
   Because the love I bore to them
   thy service easy made.
168 From strict observance of thy laws
   I never yet withdrew;
   Convinc'd that my most secret ways
   are open to thy view.

TAU.

169 To my request and earnest cry
   attend, O gracious Lord;

Inspire my heart with heav'nly skill,
   according to thy word.
170 Let my repeated pray'r at last
   before thy throne appear;
   According to thy plighted word,
   for my relief draw near.
171 Then shall my grateful lips return
   the tribute of their praise,
   When thou thy counsels hast reveal'd,
   and taught me thy just ways.
172 My tongue the praises of thy word
   shall thankfully resound,
   Because thy promises are all
   with truth and justice crown'd.
173 Let thy Almighty arm appear,
   and bring me timely aid;
   For I the laws thou hast ordain'd
   my heart's free choice have made.
174 My soul has waited long to see
   thy saving grace restor'd;
   Nor comfort knew, but what thy laws,
   thy heav'nly laws, afford.
175 Prolong my life, that I may sing
   my great Restorer's praise;
   Whose justice, from the depths of woe,
   my fainting soul shall raise.
176 Like some lost sheep I've stray'd, till I
   despair my way to find;
   Thou, therefore, Lord, thy servant seek,
   who keeps thy laws in mind.

PSALM CXX.

1 IN deep distress I oft have cry'd
      To God, who never yet deny'd
   to rescue me oppress'd with wrongs;
2 Once more, O Lord, deliv'rance send,
   From lying lips my soul defend,
   and from the rage of sland'ring tongues.
3 What little profit can accrue,
   And yet what heavy wrath is due,
   O thou perfidious tongue, to thee!
4 Thy sting upon thyself shall turn;
   Of lasting flames, that fiercely burn,
   the constant fuel thou shalt be.
5 But, O! how wretched is my doom,
   Who am a sojourner become
   in barren Mesech's desert soil!
   With Kedar's wicked tents inclos'd,
   To lawless savages expos'd,
   who live on nought but theft and spoil.

6 My

6 My hapless dwelling is with those,
　Who peace and amity oppose,
　　and pleasure take in others harms:
7 Sweet peace is all I court and seek;
　But when to them of peace I speak,
　　they straight cry out, To arms, to arms.

PSALM CXXI.

1 TO Sion's hill I lift my eyes,
　　from thence expecting aid;
2 From Sion's hill, and Sion's God
　　who heav'n and earth has made.
3 Then thou, my soul, in safety rest,
　　thy guardian will not sleep;
4 His watchful care, that Israel guards,
　　will Israel's monarch keep.
5 Shelter'd beneath th' Almighty's wings
　　thou shalt securely rest,
6 Where neither sun nor moon shall thee
　　by day or night molest.
7 From common accidents of life
　　his care shall guard thee still;
8 From the blind strokes of chance, and foes
　　that lie in wait to kill.
9 At home, abroad, in peace, in war,
　　thy God shall thee defend;
　Conduct thee through life's pilgrimage
　　safe to thy journey's end.

PSALM CXXII.

1 O 'Twas a joyful sound to hear
　　our tribes devoutly say,
　Up, Israel, to the temple haste,
　　and keep your festal day!
2 At Salem's courts we must appear,
　　with our assembled pow'rs,
3 In strong and beauteous order rang'd,
　　like her united tow'rs.
4 'Tis thither, by divine command,
　　the tribes of God repair,
　Before his ark to celebrate
　　his Name with praise and pray'r.
5 Tribunals stand erected there,
　　where equity takes place:
　There stand the courts and palaces
　　of royal David's race.
6 O, pray we then for Salem's peace,
　　for they shall prosp'rous be,
　Thou holy city of our God,
　　who bear true love to thee.

7 May peace within thy sacred walls
    a constant guest be found,
With plenty and prosperity
    thy palaces be crown'd.
8 For my dear brethren's sake, and friends
    no less than brethren dear,
I'll pray—May peace in Salem's tow'rs
    a constant guest appear.
9 But most of all I'll seek thy good,
    and ever wish thee well,
For Sion and the temple's sake,
    where God vouchsafes to dwell.

PSALM CXXIII.

1, 2 ON thee, who dwell'st above the skies,
    For mercy wait my longing eyes;
As servants wait their masters' hands,
And maids their mistresses' commands.
3, 4 O then have mercy on us, Lord;
Thy gracious aid to us afford;
To us, whom cruel foes oppress,
Grown rich and proud by our distress.

PSALM CXXIV.

1 HAD not the Lord, may Isr'el say,
    been pleas'd to interpose;
2 Had he not then espous'd our cause,
    when men against us rose;
3, 4, 5 Their wrath had swallow'd us alive,
    and rag'd without controul;
Their spite and pride's united floods
    had quite o'erwhelm'd our soul.
6 But prais'd be our eternal Lord,
    who rescu'd us that day,
Nor to their savage jaws gave up
    our threaten'd lives a prey.
7 Our soul is like a bird escap'd
    from out the fowler's net;
The snare is broke, their hopes are cross'd,
    and we at freedom set.
8 Secure in his Almighty Name
    our confidence remains,
Who, as he made both heav'n and earth,
    of both sole Monarch reigns.

PSALM CXXV.

1 WHO place on Sion's God their trust,
    like Sion's rock shall stand;
Like her immoveable be fix'd
    by his Almighty hand.

2 Look how the hills on ev'ry side
    Jerusalem inclose;
  So stands the Lord around his saints,
    to guard them from their foes.
3 The wicked may afflict the just,
    but ne'er too long oppress,
  Nor force him by despair to seek
    base means for his redress.
4 Be good, O righteous God, to those
    who righteous deeds affect;
  The heart that innocence retains,
    let innocence protect.
5 All those who walk in crooked paths,
    the Lord shall soon destroy,
  Cut off th' unjust, but crown the saints
    with lasting peace and joy.

PSALM CXXVI.

1 WHEN Sion's God her sons recall'd
      from long captivity,
  It seem'd at first a pleasing dream
    of what we wish'd to see:
2 But soon in unaccustom'd mirth,
    we did our voice employ,
  And sung our great Restorer's praise
    in thankful hymns of joy.
  Our heathen foes repining stood,
    yet were compell'd to own
  That great and wond'rous was the work
    our God for us had done.
3 " 'Twas great," say they, " 'twas wond'rous great;"
    much more should we confess,
  The Lord has done great things, whereof
    we reap the glad success.
4 To us bring back the remnant, Lord,
    of Israel's captive bands,
  More welcome than refreshing show'rs
    to parch'd and thirsty lands;
5 That we, whose work commenc'd in tears,
    may see our labours thrive,
  Till finish'd with success, to make
    our drooping hearts revive.
6 Though he desponds that sows his grain,
    yet doubtless he shall come
  To bind his full-ear'd sheaves, and bring
    the joyful harvest home.

PSALM CXXVII.

1 WE build with fruitless cost, unless
      the Lord the pile sustain:

Unless the Lord the city keep,
 the watchman wakes in vain.
2 In vain we rise before the day,
 and late to rest repair,
Allow no respite to our toil,
 and eat the bread of care.
Supplies of life, with ease to them,
 he on his saints bestows;
He crowns their labours with success,
 their nights with sound repose.
3 Children, those comforts of our life,
 are presents from the Lord;
He gives a num'rous race of heirs,
 as piety's reward.
4 As arrows in a giant's hand,
 when marching forth to war;
Ev'n so the sons of sprightly youth,
 their parents safeguard are.
5 Happy the man whose quiver's fill'd
 with these prevailing arms;
He need not fear to meet his foe,
 at law or war's alarms.

PSALM CXXVIII.

1 THE man is blest that fears the Lord,
  nor only worship pays,
But keeps his steps confin'd with care
 to his appointed ways.
2 He shall upon the sweet returns
 of his own labour feed;
Without dependence live, and see
 his wishes all succeed.
3 His wife, like a fair fertile vine,
 her lovely fruit shall bring;
His children, like young olive plants,
 about his table spring.
4 Who fears the Lord shall prosper thus;
 him Sion's God shall bless,
5 And grant him all his days to see
 Jerusalem's success.
6 He shall live on, till heirs from him
 descend with vast increase;
Much bless'd in his own prosp'rous state,
 and more in Israel's peace.

PSALM CXXIX.

1 FROM my youth up, may Israel say,
  they oft have me assail'd,
2 Reduc'd me oft to heavy straits;
 but never quite prevail'd.

3 They oft have plow'd my patient back
  with furrows deep and long;
4 But our just God has broke their chains,
  and rescu'd us from wrong.
5 Defeat, confusion, shameful rout
  be still the doom of those,
  Their righteous doom, who Sion hate,
  and Sion's God oppose.
6 Like corn upon our houses' tops,
  untimely let them fade,
  Which too much heat, and want of root,
  has blasted in the blade:
7 Which in his arms no reaper takes,
  but unregarded leaves;
  No binder thinks it worth his pains
  to fold it into sheaves.
8 No traveller that passes by
  vouchsafes a minute's stop,
  To give it one kind look, or crave
  heav'n's blessing on the crop.

PSALM CXXX.

1 FROM lowest depths of woe
  to God I sent my cry;
2 Lord, hear my supplicating voice,
  and graciously reply.
3 Should thou severely judge,
  who can the trial bear?
4 But thou forgiv'st, lest we despond,
  and quite renounce thy fear.
5 My soul with patience waits
  for thee, the living Lord;
  My hopes are on thy promise built,
  thy never-failing word.
6 My longing eyes look out
  for thy enliv'ning ray,
  More duly than the morning watch
  to spy the dawning day.
7 Let Israel trust in God,
  no bounds his mercy knows;
  The plenteous source and spring, from whence
  eternal succour flows;
8 Whose friendly streams to us
  supplies in want convey;
  A healing spring, a spring to cleanse,
  and wash our guilt away.

PSALM CXXXI.

1 O Lord, I am not proud of heart,
  nor cast a scornful eye;

Nor my aspiring thoughts employ
    in things for me too high.
2 With infant innocence thou know'st
    I have myself demean'd ;
  Compos'd to quiet, like a babe
    that from the breast is wean'd.
3 Like me let Israel hope in God,
    his aid alone implore ;
  Both now and ever trust in him,
    who lives for evermore.

PSALM CXXXII.

1 LET David, Lord, a constant place
    in thy remembrance find ;
  Let all the sorrows he endur'd
    be ever in thy mind.
2 Remember what a solemn oath
    to thee, his Lord, he swore ;
  How to the mighty God he vow'd,
    whom Jacob's sons adore ;
3, 4 I will not go into my house,
    nor to my bed ascend ;
  No soft repose shall close my eyes,
    nor sleep my eye-lids bend ;
5 Till for the Lord's design'd abode
    I mark the destin'd ground ;
  Till I a decent place of rest
    for Jacob's God have found.
6 Th' appointed place, with shouts of joy,
    at Ephrata we found,
  And made the woods and neighb'ring fields
    our glad applause resound.
7 O with due rev'rence let us then
    to his abode repair ;
  And, prostrate at his foot-stool fall'n,
    pour out our humble pray'r.
8 Arise, O Lord, and now possess
    thy constant place of rest ;
  Be that, not only with thy ark,
    but with thy presence, blest.
9, 10 Clothe thou thy priests with righteousness,
    make thou thy saints rejoice ;
  And, for thy servant David's sake,
    hear thy anointed's voice.
11 God sware to David in his truth,
    nor shall his oath be vain,
  One of thy offspring, after thee,
    upon thy throne shall reign :
12 And if thy seed my cov'nant keep,
    and to my laws submit,

Their children too upon thy throne
 for evermore shall sit.
13, 14 For Sion does, in God's esteem,
 all other seats excel;
His place of everlasting rest,
 where he desires to dwell.
15, 16 Her store, says he, I will increase,
 her poor with plenty bless;
Her saints shall shout with joy, her priests
 my saving health confess.
17 There David's pow'r shall long remain
 in his successive line,
And my anointed servant there
 shall with fresh lustre shine.
18 The faces of his vanquish'd foes
 confusion shall o'erspread;
Whilst, with confirm'd success, his crown
 shall flourish on his head.

PSALM CXXXIII.

1 HOW vast must their advantage be,
 how great their pleasure prove,
Who live like brethren, and consent
 in offices of love!
2 True love is like that precious oil,
 which, pour'd on Aaron's head,
Ran down his beard, and o'er his robes
 its costly moisture shed.
3 'Tis like refreshing dew, which does
 on Hermon's top distil;
Or like the early drops that fall
 on Sion's fruitful hill.
4 For Sion is the chosen seat,
 where the Almighty King
The promis'd blessing has ordain'd,
 and life's eternal spring.

PSALM CXXXIV.

1 BLESS God, ye servants, that attend
 upon his solemn state,
That in his temple, night by night,
 with humble rev'rence wait:
2, 3 Within his house lift up your hands,
 and bless his holy Name:
From Sion bless thy Israel, Lord,
 who earth and heav'n didst frame.

PSALM CXXXV.

1 O Praise the Lord with one consent,
 and magnify his Name;

PSALM CXXXV.

Let all the servants of the Lord
 his worthy praise proclaim.
2 Praise him all ye that in his house
 attend with constant care;
With those that to his outmost courts
 with humble zeal repair.
3 For this our truest int'rest is,
 glad hymns of praise to sing;
And with loud songs to bless his Name,
 a most delightful thing.
4 For God his own peculiar choice
 the sons of Jacob makes;
And Israel's offspring for his own
 most valu'd treasure takes.
5 That God is great, we often have
 by glad experience found;
And seen how he, with wond'rous pow'r,
 above all gods is crown'd.
6 For he, with unresisted strength,
 performs his sov'reign will,
In heav'n and earth, and wat'ry stores
 that earth's deep caverns fill.
7 He raises vapours from the ground,
 which, pois'd in liquid air,
Fall down at last in show'rs, through which
 his dreadful light'nings glare,
8 He from his store-house brings the winds;
 and he, with vengeful hand,
The first-born slew of man and beast,
 through Egypt's mourning land.
9 He dreadful signs and wonders show'd,
 through stubborn Egypt's coasts;
Nor Pharaoh could his plagues escape,
 nor all his num'rous hosts.
10, 11 'Twas he that various nations smote,
 and mighty kings suppress'd;
Sihon and Og, and all besides,
 who Canaan's land possess'd.
12, 13 Their land upon his chosen race
 he firmly did entail;
For which his fame shall always last,
 his praise shall never fail.
14 For God shall soon his peoples' cause
 with pitying eyes survey;
Repent him of his wrath, and turn
 his kindled rage away.
15 Those idols, whose false worship spreads
 o'er all the heathen lands,

Are made of silver, and of gold,
  the work of human hands.
16, 17 They move not their fictitious tongues,
  nor see with polish'd eyes;
Their counterfeited ears are deaf,
  no breath their mouth supplies.
18 As senseless as themselves are they
  that all their skill apply,
To make them, or in dang'rous times
  on them for aid rely.
19 Their just returns of thanks to God
  let grateful Israel pay;
Nor let the priests of Aaron's race
  to bless the Lord delay.
20 Their sense of his unbounded love
  let Levi's house express;
And let all those who fear the Lord,
  his Name for ever bless.
21 Let all with thanks his wond'rous works
  in Sion's courts proclaim;
Let them in Salem, where he dwells,
  exalt his holy Name.

PSALM CXXXVI.

1 TO God the mighty Lord
    Your joyful thanks repeat;
  To him due praise afford,
    As good as he is great:
      For God does prove
      Our constant friend,
      His boundless love
      Shall never end.
2, 3 To him, whose wond'rous pow'r
  All other gods obey,
  Whom earthly kings adore,
  This grateful homage pay:
      For God &c.
4, 5 By his Almighty hand
  Amazing works are wrought;
  The heav'ns by his command
  Were to perfection brought:
      For God &c.
6 He spread the ocean round
  About the spacious land;
  And made the rising ground
  Above the waters stand:
      For God &c.
7, 8, 9 Through heav'n he did display
  His num'rous hosts of light;

The

  The sun to rule by day,
  The moon and stars by night:
   For God &c.
10, 11, 12 He struck the first-born dead
  Of Egypt's stubborn land;
  And thence his people led
  With his resistless hand:
   For God &c.
13, 14 By him the raging sea,
  As if in pieces rent,
  Disclos'd a middle way,
  Through which his people went:
   For God &c.
15 Where soon he overthrew
  Proud Pharaoh and his host,
  Who, daring to pursue,
  Were in the billows lost:
   For God &c.
16, 17, 18 Through deserts vast and wild
  He led the chosen seed;
  And famous princes foil'd,
  And made great monarchs bleed:
   For God &c.
19, 20 Sihon, whose potent hand
  Great Ammon's sceptre sway'd;
  And Og, whose stern command
  Rich Bashan's land obey'd:
   For God &c.
21, 22 And, of his wond'rous grace,
  Their lands, whom he destroy'd,
  He gave to Israel's race,
  To be by them enjoy'd:
   For God &c.
23, 24 He, in our depth of woes,
  On us with favour thought,
  And from our cruel foes
  In peace and safety brought:
   For God &c.
25, 26 He does the food supply,
  On which all creatures live:
  To God, who reigns on high,
  Eternal praises give:
    For God will prove
    Our constant friend,
    His boundless love
    Shall never end.

PSALM CXXXVII.

1 WHEN we, our weary limbs to rest,
  Sat down by proud Euphrates' stream,

PSALM CXXXVIII.

We wept, with doleful thoughts oppreſt,
    and Sion was our mournful theme.
2 Our harps, that when with joy we ſung,
    were wont their tuneful parts to bear,
With ſilent ſtrings neglected hung
    on willow-trees, that wither'd there.
3 Mean while our foes, who all conſpir'd
    to triumph in our ſlaviſh wrongs,
Muſic and mirth of us requir'd,
    " Come, ſing us one of Sion's ſongs."
4 How ſhall we tune our voice to ſing,
    or touch our harps with ſkilful hands?
Shall hymns of joy to God, our King,
    be ſung by ſlaves in foreign lands?
5 O Salem, our once happy ſeat!
    when I of thee forgetful prove,
Let then my trembling hand forget
    the ſpeaking ſtrings with art to move!
6 If I to mention thee forbear,
    eternal ſilence ſeize my tongue;
Or if I ſing one chearful air,
    till thy deliv'rance is my ſong.
7 Remember, Lord, how Edom's race,
    in thy own city's fatal day,
Cry'd out, " Her ſtately walls deface,
    " and with the ground quite level lay."
8 Proud Babel's daughter, doom'd to be
    of grief and woe the wretched prey;
Bleſs'd is the man who ſhall to thee
    the wrongs thou laid'ſt on us repay.
9 Thrice bleſs'd, who, with juſt rage poſſeſt,
    and deaf to all the parents' moans,
Shall ſnatch thy infants from the breaſt,
    and daſh their heads againſt the ſtones.

PSALM CXXXVIII.

1 WITH my whole heart, my God and King,
    thy praiſe I will proclaim;
Before the gods with joy I'll ſing,
    and bleſs thy holy Name.
2 I'll worſhip at thy ſacred ſeat,
    and, with thy love inſpir'd,
The praiſes of thy truth repeat,
    o'er all thy works admir'd.
3 Thou graciouſly inclin'dſt thine ear,
    when I to thee did cry;
And when my ſoul was preſs'd with fear,
    didſt inward ſtrength ſupply.

4 Therefore shall ev'ry earthly prince
   thy Name with praise pursue;
  Whom these admir'd events convince
   that all thy works are true.
5 They all thy wond'rous ways, O Lord,
   with chearful songs shall bless;
  And all thy glorious acts record;
   thy awful pow'r confess.
6 For God, although enthron'd on high,
   does thence the poor respect;
  The proud far off his scornful eye
   beholds with just neglect.
7 Though I with troubles am oppress'd,
   he shall my foes disarm,
  Relieve my soul when most distress'd,
   and keep me safe from harm.
8 The Lord, whose mercies ever last,
   shall fix my happy state;
  And, mindful of his favours past,
   shall his own work compleat.

PSALM CXXXIX.

1, 2 THOU, Lord, by strictest search hast known
     My rising up and lying down;
  My secret thoughts are known to thee,
  Known long before conceiv'd by me.
3 Thine eye my bed and path surveys,
  My public haunts and private ways;
4 Thou know'st what 'tis my lips would vent,
  My yet unutter'd words' intent.
5 Surrounded by thy pow'r I stand;
  On ev'ry side I find thy hand:
6 O skill, for human reach too high!
  Too dazzling bright for mortal eye!
7 O could I so perfidious be,
  To think of once deserting thee,
  Where, Lord, could I thy influence shun?
  Or whither from thy presence run?
8 If up to heav'n I take my flight,
  'Tis there thou dwell'st enthron'd in light;
  If down to hell's infernal plains,
  'Tis there Almighty vengeance reigns.
9 If I the morning's wings could gain,
  And fly beyond the western main,
10 Thy swifter hand would first arrive,
  And there arrest thy fugitive.
11 Or, should I try to shun thy sight,
  Beneath the sable wings of night;
  One glance from thee, one piercing ray,
  Would kindle darkness into day.

12 The veil of night is no disguise,
   No screen from thy all-searching eyes;
   Through midnight shades thou find'st thy way,
   As in the blazing noon of day.
13 Thou know'st the texture of my heart,
   My reins, and ev'ry vital part;
   Each single thread in nature's loom,
   By thee was cover'd in the womb.
14 I'll praise thee, from whose hands I came,
   A work of such a curious frame;
   The wonders thou in me hast shown,
   My soul with grateful joy must own.
15 Thine eyes my substance did survey,
   Whilst yet a lifeless mass it lay,
   In secret how exactly wrought,
   Ere from its dark inclosure brought.
16 Thou didst the shapeless embryo see,
   Its parts were register'd by thee;
   Thou saw'st the daily growth they took,
   Form'd by the model of thy book.
17 Let me acknowledge too, O God,
   That, since this maze of life I trod,
   Thy thoughts of love to me surmount
   The pow'r of numbers to recount.
18 Far sooner could I reckon o'er
   The sands upon the ocean's shore;
   Each morn revising what I've done,
   I find th' account but new begun.
19 The wicked thou shalt slay, O God:
   Depart from me, ye men of blood,
20 Whose tongues heav'n's majesty profane,
   And take th' Almighty's Name in vain.
21 Lord, hate not I their impious crew,
   Who thee with enmity pursue?
   And does not grief my heart oppress,
   When reprobates thy laws transgress?
22 Who practise enmity to thee
   Shall utmost hatred have from me;
   Such men I utterly detest,
   As if they were my foes profest.
23, 24 Search, try, O God, my thoughts and heart,
   If mischief lurk in any part;
   Correct me where I go astray,
   And guide me in thy perfect way.

PSALM CXL.

1 PReserve me, Lord, from crafty foes,
   of treacherous intent;
2 And from the sons of violence,
   on open mischief bent.

3 Their sland'ring tongue the serpent's sting
    in sharpness does exceed;
  Between their lips the gall of asps
    and adders' venom breed.
4 Preserve me, Lord, from wicked hands,
    nor leave my soul forlorn,
  A prey to sons of violence,
    who have my ruin sworn.
5 The proud for me have laid their snare,
    and spread their wily net;
  With traps and gins, where'er I move,
    I find my steps beset.
6 But thus environ'd with distress,
    thou art my God, I said;
  Lord, hear my supplicating voice,
    that calls to thee for aid.
7 O Lord, the God whose saving strength
    kind succour did convey,
  And cover'd my advent'rous head
    in battle's doubtful day;
8 Permit not their unjust designs
    to answer their desire;
  Lest they, encourag'd by success,
    to bolder crimes aspire.
9 Let first their chiefs the sad effects
    of their injustice mourn;
  The blast of their envenom'd breath
    upon themselves return.
10 Let them who kindle first the flame,
    its sacrifice become;
  The pit they digg'd for me be made
    their own untimely tomb.
11 Though slander's breath may raise a storm,
    it quickly will decay;
  Their rage does but the torrent swell,
    that bears themselves away.
12 God will assert the poor man's cause,
    and speedy succour give:
  The just shall celebrate his praise,
    and in his presence live.

PSALM CXLI.

1 TO thee, O Lord, my cries ascend,
    O haste to my relief;
  And with accustom'd pity hear
    the accents of my grief.
2 Instead of off'rings, let my pray'r
    like morning incense rise;

My lifted hand supply the place
      of ev'ning sacrifice.
3 From hasty language curb my tongue,
      and let a constant guard
   Still keep the portal of my lips
      with wary silence barr'd.
4 From wicked mens' designs and deeds
      my heart and hands restrain;
   Nor let me in the booty share
      of their unrighteous gain.
5 Let upright men reprove my faults,
      and I shall think them kind;
   Like balm that heals a wounded head
      I their reproof shall find;
   And, in return, my fervant pray'r
      I shall for them address,
   When they are tempted and reduc'd,
      like me, to sore distress.
6 When sculking in Engedi's rock,
      I to their chiefs appeal,
   If one reproachful word I spoke,
      when I had pow'r to kill.
7 Yet us they persecute to death;
      our scatter'd ruins lie
   As thick as from the hewer's axe
      the fever'd splinters fly.
8 But, Lord, to thee I still direct
      my supplicating eyes,
   O leave not destitute my soul,
      whose trust on thee relies.
9 Do thou preserve me from the snares
      that wicked hands have laid;
   Let them in their own nets be caught,
      while my escape is made.

PSALM CXLII.

1 TO God, with mournful voice,
      in deep distress I pray'd;
2 Made him the umpire of my cause,
      my wrongs before him laid.
3 Thou didst my steps direct,
      when my griev'd soul despair'd;
   For where I thought to walk secure
      they had their traps prepar'd.
4 I look'd, but found no friend
      to own me in distress;
   All refuge fail'd, no man vouchsaf'd
      his pity or redress.

5 To God at laft I pray'd;
　　thou, Lord, my refuge art,
　My portion in the land of life,
　　till life itfelf depart.
6 Reduc'd to greateft ftraits,
　　to thee I make my moan;
　O fave me from oppreffing foes,
　　for me too pow'rful grown.
7 That I may praife thy Name,
　　my foul from prifon bring;
　Whilft of thy kind regard to me
　　affembled faints fhall fing.

PSALM CXLIII.

1 LORD, hear my pray'r, and to my cry
　　thy wonted audience lend;
　In thy accuftom'd faith and truth
　　a gracious anfwer fend.
2 Nor at thy ftrict tribunal bring
　　thy fervant to be try'd;
　For in thy fight no living man
　　can e'er be juftify'd.
3 The fpiteful foe purfues my life,
　　whofe comforts all are fled;
　He drives me into caves as dark
　　as manfions of the dead.
4 My fpirit therefore is o'erwhelm'd,
　　and finks within my breaft;
　My mournful heart grows defolate,
　　with heavy woes oppreft.
5 I call to mind the days of old,
　　and wonders thou haft wrought:
　My former dangers and efcapes
　　employ my mufing thought.
6 To thee my hands in humble pray'r
　　I fervently ftretch out;
　My foul for thy refreshment thirfts,
　　like land opprefs'd with drought.
7 Hear me with fpeed; my fpirit fails;
　　thy face no longer hide,
　Left I become forlorn, like them
　　that in the grave refide.
8 Thy kindnefs early let me hear,
　　whofe truft on thee depends;
　Teach me the way where I fhould go;
　　my foul to thee afcends.
9 Do thou, O Lord, from all my foes
　　preferve and fet me free;
　A fafe retreat againft their rage
　　my foul implores from thee.

10 Thou

PSALM CXLIV.

10 Thou art my God, thy righteous will
    inftruct me to obey;
Let thy good fpirit lead and keep
    my foul in thy right way.
11 O! for the fake of thy great Name,
    revive my drooping heart;
For thy truth's fake, to me, diftrefs'd,
    thy promis'd aid impart.
12 In pity to my fuff'rings, Lord,
    reduce my foes to fhame;
Slay them that perfecute a foul
    devoted to thy Name.

PSALM CXLIV.

1 FOR ever blefs'd be God the Lord,
    who does his needful aid impart,
At once both ftrength and fkill afford,
    to wield my arms with warlike art.
2 His goodnefs is my fort and tow'r,
    my ftrong deliv'rance and my fhield;
In him I truft, whofe matchlefs pow'r
    makes to my fway fierce nations yield.
3 Lord, what's in man, that thou fhould'ft love
    of him fuch tender care to take?
What in his offspring could thee move
    fuch great account of him to make?
4 The life of man does quickly fade,
    his thoughts but empty are and vain,
His days are like a flying fhade,
    of whofe fhort ftay no figns remain.
5 In folemn ftate, O God, defcend,
    whilft heav'n its lofty head inclines;
The fmoaking hills afunder rend,
    of thy approach the awful figns.
6 Difcharge thy awful light'nings round,
    and make thy fcatter'd foes retreat;
Then with thy pointed arrows wound,
    and their deftruction foon compleat.
7, 8 Do thou, O Lord, from heav'n engage
    thy boundlefs pow'r my foes to quell,
And fnatch me from the ftormy rage
    of threat'ning waves, that proudly fwell.
Fight thou againft my foreign foes,
    who utter fpeeches falfe and vain;
Who, though in folemn leagues they clofe,
    their fworn engagements ne'er maintain.
9 So I to thee, O King of kings,
    in new-made hymns my voice fhall raife,
And inftruments of many ftrings
    fhall help me thus to fing thy praife:

10 " God

10 "God does to kings his aid afford,
    "to them his sure salvation sends;
    "'Tis he that from the murd'ring sword
    "his servant David still defends."
11 Fight thou against my foreign foes,
    who utter speeches false and vain;
   Who, though in solemn leagues they close,
    their sworn engagements ne'er maintain.
12 Then our young sons like trees shall grow,
    well planted in some fruitful place;
   Our daughters shall like pillars show,
    design'd some royal court to grace.
13 Our garners, fill'd with various store,
    shall us and ours with plenty feed;
   Our sheep, increasing more and more,
    shall thousands and ten thousands breed.
14 Strong shall our lab'ring oxen grow,
    nor in their constant labour faint;
   Whilst we no war nor slav'ry know,
    and in our streets hear no complaint.
15 Thrice happy is that people's case,
    whose various blessings thus abound;
   Who God's true worship still embrace,
    and are with his protection crown'd.

PSALM CXLV.

1, 2 THEE I will bless, my God and King,
    thy endless praise proclaim;
   This tribute daily I will bring,
    and ever bless thy Name.
3 Thou, Lord, beyond compare art great,
    and highly to be prais'd;
   Thy majesty, with boundless height,
    above our knowledge rais'd.
4 Renown'd for mighty acts, thy fame
    to future time extends;
   From age to age thy glorious name
    successively descends.
5, 6 Whilst I thy glory and renown,
    and wond'rous works express,
   The world with me thy might shall own,
    and thy great pow'r confess.
7 The praise that to thy love belongs,
    they shall with joy proclaim;
   Thy truth of all their grateful songs
    shall be the constant theme.
8 The Lord is good; fresh acts of grace
    his pity still supplies:
   His anger moves with slowest pace,
    his willing mercy flies.

9, 10 Thy

PSALM CXLVI.

9, 10 Thy love through earth extends its fame,
    to all thy works expreſt;
Theſe ſhow thy praiſe, whilſt thy great Name
    is by thy ſervants bleſt.
11 They, with a glorious proſpect fir'd,
    ſhall of thy kingdoms ſpeak;
And thy great pow'r, by all admir'd,
    their lofty ſubject make.
12 God's glorious works of ancient date
    ſhall thus to all be known;
And thus his kingdom's royal ſtate
    with public ſplendor ſhown.
13 His ſtedfaſt throne, from changes free,
    ſhall ſtand for ever faſt;
His boundleſs ſway no end ſhall ſee,
    but time itſelf out-laſt.

PART II.

14, 15 The Lord does them ſupport that fall,
    and makes the proſtrate riſe;
For his kind aid all creatures call,
    who timely food ſupplies.
16 Whate'er their various wants require,
    with open hand he gives;
And ſo fulfils the juſt deſire
    of ev'ry thing that lives.
17, 18 How holy is the Lord, how juſt,
    how righteous all his ways!
How nigh to him, who with firm truſt
    for his aſſiſtance prays!
19 He grants the full deſires of thoſe
    who him with fear adore;
And will their troubles ſoon compoſe,
    when they his aid implore.
20 The Lord preſerves all thoſe with care
    whom grateful love employs;
But ſinners, who his vengeance dare,
    with furious rage deſtroys.
21 My time to come, in praiſes ſpent,
    ſhall ſtill advance his fame;
And all mankind with one conſent,
    for ever bleſs his Name.

PSALM CXLVI.

1, 2 O Praiſe the Lord, and thou, my ſoul,
    for ever bleſs his Name:
His wond'rous love, while life ſhall laſt,
    my conſtant praiſe ſhall claim.
3 On kings, the greateſt ſons of men,
    let none for aid rely;

They cannot save in dang'rous times,
    nor timely help apply.
4 Depriv'd of breath, to dust they turn,
    and there neglected lie;
And all their thoughts and vain designs
    together with them die.
5 Then happy he, who Jacob's God
    for his protector takes;
Who still, with well-plac'd hope, the Lord
    his constant refuge makes.
6 The Lord, who made both heav'n and earth,
    and all that they contain,
Will never quit his stedfast truth,
    nor make his promise vain.
7 The poor, oppreſt, from all their wrongs
    are eas'd by his decree;
He gives the hungry needful food,
    and sets the pris'ners free.
8 By him the blind receive their sight,
    the weak and fall'n he rears;
With kind regard and tender love
    he for the righteous cares.
9 The strangers he preserves from harm,
    the orphan kindly treats;
Defends the widow, and the wiles
    of wicked men defeats.
10 The God that does in Sion dwell
    is our eternal King:
From age to age his reign endures:
    let all his praises sing.

PSALM CXLVII.

1 O Praise the Lord with hymns of joy,
    and celebrate his fame!
For pleasant, good, and comely 'tis
    to praise his holy Name.
2 His holy city God will build,
    though levell'd with the ground;
Bring back his people, though dispers'd
    through all the nations round.
3, 4 He kindly heals the broken hearts,
    and all their wounds does close;
He tells the number of the stars,
    their sev'ral names he knows.
5, 6 Great is the Lord, and great his pow'r,
    his wisdom has no bound;
The meek he raises, and throws down
    the wicked to the ground.

7 To God, the Lord, a hymn of praise
    with grateful voices sing;
  To songs of triumph tune the harp,
    and strike each warbling string.
8 He covers heav'n with clouds, and thence
    refreshing rain bestows;
  Through him, on mountain-tops, the grass
    with wond'rous plenty grows.
9 He savage beasts that loosely range,
    with timely food supplies;
  He feeds the ravens' tender brood,
    and stops their hungry cries.
10 He values not the warlike steed,
    but does his strength disdain;
  The nimble foot that swiftly runs
    no prize from him can gain.
11 But he to him that fears his Name
    his tender love extends;
  To him that on his boundless grace
    with stedfast hope depends.
12, 13 Let Sion and Jerusalem
    to God their praise address;
  Who fenc'd their gates with massy bars,
    and does their children bless.
14, 15 Through all their borders he gives peace,
    with finest wheat they're fed;
  He speaks the word, and what he wills
    is done as soon as said.
16 Large flakes of snow, like fleecy wool,
    descend at his command;
  And hoary frost, like ashes spread,
    is scatter'd o'er the land.
17 When, join'd to these, he does his hail
    in little morsels break,
  Who can against his piercing cold
    secure defences make?
18 He sends his word, which melts the ice;
    he makes his wind to blow;
  And soon the streams, congeal'd before,
    in plenteous currents flow.
19 By him his statutes and decrees
    to Jacob's sons were shown;
  And still to Israel's chosen seed
    his righteous laws are known.
20 No other nation this can boast;
    nor did he e'er afford
  To heathen lands his oracles,
    and knowledge of his word.

PSALM

PSALM CXLVIII.

1, 2 YE boundless realms of joy,
Exalt your Maker's fame;
His praise your song employ
Above the starry frame:
 Your voices raise,
 Ye Cherubim,
 And Seraphim,
 To sing his praise.

3, 4 Thou moon, that rul'st the night,
And sun that guid'st the day,
Ye glitt'ring stars of light,
To him your homage pay:
 His praise declare,
 Ye heav'ns above,
 And clouds that move
 In liquid air.

5, 6 Let them adore the Lord,
And praise his holy Name,
By whose Almighty word
They all from nothing came:
 And all shall last,
 From changes free;
 His firm decree
 Stands ever fast.

7, 8 Let earth her tribute pay;
Praise him ye dreadful whales,
And fish that through the sea
Glide swift with glitt'ring scales;
 Fire, hail, and snow,
 And misty air,
 And winds that, where
 He bids them, blow.

9, 10 By hills and mountains, all
In grateful concert join'd;
By cedars stately tall,
And trees for fruit design'd;
 By ev'ry beast,
 And creeping thing,
 And fowl of wing,
 His Name be blest.

11, 12 Let all of royal birth,
With those of humbler frame,
And judges of the earth,
His matchless praise proclaim:
 In this design,
 Let youths with maids,
 And hoary heads
 With children join.

13 United

13 United zeal be shown,
   His wond'rous fame to raise,
   Whose glorious Name alone
   Deserves our endless praise:
     Earth's utmost ends
     His pow'r obey;
     His glorious sway
     The sky transcends.
14 His chosen saints to grace,
   He sets them up on high,
   And favours Israel's race,
   Who still to him are nigh:
     O therefore raise,
     Your grateful voice,
     And still rejoice
     The Lord to praise.

PSALM CXLIX.

1, 2 O Praise ye the Lord,
       prepare your glad voice,
   His praise in the great
     assembly to sing:
   In our great Creator
     let Israel rejoice;
   And children of Sion
     be glad in their King.
3, 4 Let them his great Name
       extol in the dance;
   With timbrel and harp
     his praises express;
   Who always takes pleasure
     his saints to advance,
   And with his salvation
     the humble to bless.
5, 6 With glory adorn'd,
     his people shall sing
   To God, who their beds
     with safety does shield;
   Their mouths fill'd with praises
     of him, their great King;
   Whilst a two-edged sword
     their right-hand shall wield;
7, 8 Just vengeance to take
     for injuries past;
   To punish those lands
     for ruin design'd;
   With chains, as their captives,
     to tie their kings fast,
   With fetters of iron
     their nobles to bind.

9 Thus

9 Thus shall they make good,
    when them they destroy,
  The dreadful decree
    which God does proclaim:
  Such honour and triumph
    his saints shall enjoy:
  O therefore for ever
    exalt his great Name.

PSALM CL.

1 O Praise the Lord in that blest place,
    from whence his goodness largely flows;
  Praise him in heav'n, where he his face,
    unveil'd, in perfect glory shows.
2 Praise him for all the mighty acts,
    which he in our behalf has done;
  His kindness this return exacts,
    with which our praise should equal run.
3 Let the shrill trumpet's warlike voice
    make rocks and hills his praise rebound;
  Praise him with harp's melodious noise,
    and gentle psalt'ry's silver sound.
4 Let virgin troops soft timbrels bring,
    and some with graceful motion dance;
  Let instruments of various strings,
    with organs join'd, his praise advance.
5 Let them who joyful hymns compose,
    to symbals set their songs of praise;
  Cymbals of common use, and those
    that loudly sound on solemn days.
6 Let all that vital breath enjoy,
    the breath he does to them afford,
  In just returns of praise employ:
    let ev'ry creature praise the Lord.

GLORIA PATRI.

Common Measure.

TO Father, Son, and Holy Ghost,
    the God whom we adore,
  Be glory, as it was, is now,
    and shall be evermore.

As Psalm XXV.

To God the Father, Son,
    and Spirit, glory be;
  As 'twas, and is, and shall be so
    to all eternity.

GLORIA PATRI.

As Psalm C.

To Father, Son, and Holy Ghost,
   the God whom earth and heav'n adore,
Be glory, as it was of old,
   is now, and shall be evermore.

As Psalm XXXVII.

To Father, Son, and Holy Ghost,
The God whom heav'n's triumphant host,
   and suff'ring saints on earth adore,
Be glory, as in ages past,
As now it is, and so shall last,
   when time itself shall be no more.

As Psalm CXLVIII.

To God the Father, Son,
And Spirit ever bless'd,
Eternal three in one,
All worship be address'd;
   As heretofore
   It was, is now,
   And shall be so
     For evermore.

As Psalm CXLIX.

By Angels in heav'n
   of ev'ry degree,
And saints upon earth,
   all praise be address'd
To God in three persons,
   one God ever bless'd;
As it has been, now is,
   and always shall be.

The SONG of the ANGELS.

For the NATIVITY *of our bleſſed* LORD *and* SAVIOUR.
   Luke II. *ver.* 8—15.

1. WHile ſhepherds watch'd their flocks by night,
       all ſeated on the ground,
   The angel of the Lord came down,
       and glory ſhone around.
2. " Fear not," ſaid he, for mighty dread
       had ſeiz'd their troubled mind ;
   " Glad tidings of great joy I bring
   " to you, and all mankind.
3. " To you, in David's Town, this day
   " is born of David's line,
   " The Saviour, who is Chriſt the Lord ;
   " and this ſhall be the ſign :
4. " The Heav'nly Babe you there ſhall find,
   " to human view diſplay'd,
   " All meanly wrapp'd in ſwathing bands,
   " and in a manger laid."
5. Thus ſpake the Seraph, and forthwith
       appear'd a ſhining throng
   Of Angels, praiſing God, who thus
       addreſs'd their joyful ſong :
6. " All glory be to God on high,
   " and to the earth be peace :
   " Good will, henceforth, from heav'n to men
   " begin, and never ceaſe."

HYMN II.

The SONG *of* MEN, *reſponſive to the* SONG
        of the ANGELS.

1. WHILE Angels thus, O Lord, rejoice,
       ſhall men no Anthem raiſe ?
   O may we loſe theſe uſeleſs tongues,
       when we forget to praiſe !
2. Then let us ſwell reſponſive notes,
       and join the heav'nly throng ;
   For Angels no ſuch love have known
       as we, to wake their ſong.
3. Good-will to ſinful duſt is ſhown,
       and peace on earth is giv'n ;
   For lo ! th' incarnate Saviour comes,
       with news of joy from heav'n !

4 Mercy

4 Mercy and truth, with sweet accord,
　　his rising beams adorn;
　Let heav'n and earth in concert sing—
　　"The Promis'd Child is born!"
5 Glory to God, in highest strains,
　　by highest worlds is paid;
　Be glory, then, by us proclaim'd,
　　and by our lives display'd;
6 Till we attain those blissful realms,
　　where now our Saviour reigns;
　To rival these celestial Choirs
　　in their immortal strains!

HYMN III.
For GOOD-FRIDAY.
On the Sufferings of our blessed Lord and Saviour.

1 FROM whence these direful omens round,
　　which heav'n and earth amaze?
　Wherefore do earthquakes cleave the ground?
　　why hides the sun his rays?
2 Well may the earth astonish'd shake,
　　and nature sympathize!
　The sun as darkest night be black!
　　their Maker, Jesus dies!
3 Behold fast streaming from the tree
　　his all-atoning blood!
　Is this the Infinite? 'tis he,
　　my Saviour and my God!
4 For me these pangs his soul assail,
　　for me this death is borne;
　My sins gave sharpness to the nail,
　　and pointed ev'ry thorn.
5 Let sin no more my soul enslave,
　　break, Lord, its tyrant chain;
　O save me, whom thou cam'st to save,
　　nor bleed, nor die in vain!

HYMN IV.
For EASTER-DAY.
On the Resurrection.

1 SINCE Christ our Passover is slain,
　　a sacrifice for all;
　Let all, with thankful hearts, agree
　　to keep the Festival:
2 Not with the leaven, as of old,
　　of sin and malice fed;
　But with unfeign'd sincerity,
　　and truth's unleaven'd bread.

3 Christ being rais'd by Pow'r Divine,
   and rescu'd from the grave,
  Shall die no more; Death shall on him
   no more dominion have.
4 For that he died, 'twas for our sins
   he once vouchsaf'd to die:
  But that he lives, he lives to God
   for all eternity.
5 So count yourselves as dead to sin,
   but graciously restor'd;
  And made, henceforth, alive to God,
   through Jesus Christ our Lord.

HYMN V.
For the same.

1 CHrist from the dead is rais'd, and made
   the First Fruits of the tomb;
  For, as by man came death, by man
   did resurrection come.
2 For, as in Adam all mankind
   did guilt and death derive;
  So, by the righteousness of Christ,
   shall all be made alive.
3 If then ye risen are with Christ,
   seek only how to get
  The things which are above, where Christ
   at God's right-hand is set.

HYMN VI.
For WHITSUNDAY.

1 COME, Holy Ghost! Creator, come,
   inspire the souls of thine;
  Till ev'ry heart which thou hast made
   be fill'd with grace divine.
2 Thou art the Comforter, the gift
   of God, and fire of love;
  The everlasting spring of joy,
   and unction from above.
3 Thy gifts are manifold, thou writ'st
   God's law in each true heart;
  The Promise of the Father, thou
   dost heav'nly speech impart.
4 Enlighten our dark souls, till they
   thy sacred love embrace;
  Assist our minds, by nature frail,
   with thy celestial grace.
5 Drive far from us the mortal foe,
   and give us peace within,

That,

That, by thy guidance bleſt, we may
  eſcape the ſnares of ſin.
5 Teach us the Father to confeſs,
  and Son, from death reviv'd,
And thee with both, O Holy Ghoſt!
  who art from both deriv'd.

HYMN VII.
For the ſame.

1 COME, Holy Spirit, Heav'nly Dove,
    with all thy quick'ning pow'rs;
  Kindle a flame of ſacred love,
    In theſe cold hearts of ours.

2 See how we grovel here below,
    fond of theſe earthly toys;
  Our ſouls, how heavily they go,
    to reach eternal joys!

3 In vain we tune our lifeleſs ſongs,
    in vain we ſtrive to riſe!
  Hoſannas languiſh on our tongues,
    and our devotion dies.

4 Come, Holy Spirit, Heav'nly Dove,
    with all thy quick'ning pow'rs,
  Come, ſhed abroad a Saviour's love,
    and that ſhall kindle ours!

HYMN VIII.
For the ſame.

1 HE's come! let every knee be bent,
    all hearts new joy reſume;
  Sing, ye redeem'd, with one conſent,
    "The Comforter is come."

2 What greater gift, what greater love,
    could God on man beſtow?
  Angels for this rejoice above,
    let man rejoice below!

3 Hail, Bleſſed Spirit! may each ſoul
    thy ſacred influence feel;
  Do thou each ſinful thought controul,
    and fix our wav'ring zeal!

4 Thou to the conſcience doſt convey
    thoſe checks which we ſhould know;
  Thy motions point to us the way;
    thou giv'ſt us ſtrength to go.

HYMN IX.
For the HOLY COMMUNION.
From the Revelation of St. John.

1 *THOU, God, all glory, honour, pow'r,
    art worthy to receive;

* Chap. iv.

Since all things by thy pow'r were made,
  and by thy bounty live.
2 †And worthy is the Lamb all pow'r,
  honour, and wealth to gain,
 Glory and strength ; who, for our sins,
  a sacrifice was slain !
3 ‡All worthy thou, who hast redeem'd,
  and ransom'd us to God,
 From ev'ry nation, ev'ry coast,
  by thy most precious blood.
4 ‖ Blessing and honour, glory, pow'r,
  by all in earth and heav'n,
 To him that sits upon the throne,
  and to the Lamb be giv'n.

HYMN X.
For the same.

1 MY God, and is thy Table spread ?
  and does thy Cup with love o'erflow ?
 Thither be all thy children led,
  and let them thy sweet mercies know !
2 Hail sacred Feast, which Jesus makes !
  rich banquet of his flesh and blood !
 Thrice happy he who here partakes
  that sacred stream, that heav'nly food !
3 Why are its dainties all in vain
  before unwilling hearts display'd ?
 Was not for you the victim slain ?
  are you forbid the children's bread ?
4 O let thy table honour'd be,
  and furnish'd well with joyful guests ;
 And may each soul salvation see,
  that here its holy pledges tastes !
5 Drawn by the quick'ning grace, O Lord !
  in countless numbers let them come,
 And gather from their Father's board,
  the bread that lives beyond the tomb !
6 Nor let thy spreading Gospel rest,
  till through the world thy truth has run,
 Till with this bread all men be blest
  who see the light, or feel the sun !

HYMN XI.
For the same.

1 AND are we now brought near to God,
   who once at distance stood ?
 And, to effect this glorious change,
  did Jesus shed his blood ?
2 O for a song of ardent praise,
  to bear our souls above !

What

† *Chap.* v. 12.   ‡ *Chap.* v. 9.   ‖ *Ver.* 13.

What should allay our lively hope,
   or damp our flaming love!
3 Then let us join the heav'nly Choirs,
   to praise our Heav'nly King!
   O may that love which spread this board,
   inspire us while we sing—
4 " Glory to God in highest strains,
   " and to the earth be peace;
   " Good-will from heav'n to men is come;
   " and let it never cease!"

HYMN XII.
On the NEW-YEAR.

1 THE God of life, whose constant care
    With blessings crowns each op'ning year,
My scanty span doth still prolong,
And wakes anew mine annual song.
2 How many precious souls are fled
To the vast regions of the dead,
Since to this day the changing sun
Through his last yearly period run.
3 We yet survive; but who can say,
   " Or through this year, or month, or day,
   " I shall retain this vital breath,
   " Thus far, at least, in league with death?"
4 That breath is thine, Eternal God;
'Tis thine to fix my soul's abode;
It holds its life from thee alone,
On earth, or in the world unknown.
5 To thee our spirits we resign,
Make them and own them still as thine;
So shall they live secure from fear,
Though death should blast the rising year.
6 Thy children, panting to be gone,
May bid the tide of time roll on,
To land them on that happy shore,
Where years and death are known no more!
7 No more fatigue, no more distress,
Nor sin nor hell shall reach that place;
No groans to mingle with the songs,
Resounding from immortal tongues:
8 No more alarms from ghostly foes;
No cares to break the long repose;
No midnight shade, no clouded sun,
But sacred, high, eternal noon.
9 O, long expected year! begin;
Dawn on this world of woe and sin;
Fain would we leave this weary road,
To sleep in death, and rest with God.

HYMN XIII.
The Christian's HOPE.

1 WHEN, rising from the bed of death,
    o'erwhelm'd with guilt and fear,
I see my Maker, face to face;
    O how shall I appear!

2 If yet, while pardon may be found,
    and mercy may be sought,
My heart with inward horror shrinks,
    and trembles at the thought;

3 When thou, O Lord, shalt stand disclos'd
    in Majesty severe,
And sit in judgment on my soul;
    O how shall I appear!

4 But thou hast told the troubled mind,
    who does her sins lament;
The timely tribute of her tears
    shall endless woe prevent.

5 Then see the sorrow of my heart,
    e'er yet it be too late;
And hear my Saviour's dying groans,
    to give these sorrows weight.

6 For never shall my soul despair
    her pardon to procure,
Who knows thy only Son has died,
    to make her pardon sure.

7 Great God! with wonder and with praise
    on all thy works I look;
But still thy wisdom, pow'r, and grace,
    shine brighter in thy Book.

8 The stars, that in their courses roll,
    have much instruction giv'n;
But thy good Word informs my soul
    how I may soar to heav'n.

9 The fields provide me food, and show
    the goodness of the Lord;
But fruits of life and glory grow
    in thy most holy Word.

10 Here are my choicest treasures hid,
    here my best comfort lies;
Here my desires are satisfy'd,
    and here my hopes arise.

11 Lord, make me understand thy law,
    show what my faults have been;
And from thy Gospel let me draw
    pardon for all my sin.

12 Here would I learn how Christ has died
    to save my soul from hell;

Not all the books on earth beside
    such heav'nly wonders tell.
13 Then let me love my Bible more,
    and take a fresh delight,
By day to read these wonders o'er,
    and meditate by night.

HYMN XIV.
On Gratitude to GOD.

1 WHEN all thy mercies, O my God,
    my rising soul surveys;
Transported with the view, I'm lost
    in wonder, love, and praise!

2 O how shall words with equal warmth
    the gratitude declare,
That glows within my ravish'd heart?
    but thou canst read it there.

3 Thy Providence my life sustain'd,
    and all my wants redrest,
When in the silent womb I lay,
    and hung upon the breast.

4 To all my weak complaints and cries
    thy mercy lent an ear,
Ere yet my feeble thoughts had learnt
    to form themselves in pray'r

5 Unnumber'd comforts to my soul
    thy tender care bestow'd,
Before my infant heart conceiv'd
    from whom those comforts flow'd.

6 When in the slipp'ry paths of youth
    with heedless steps I ran,
Thine arm, unseen, convey'd me safe,
    and led me up to man.

7 Through hidden dangers, toils, and deaths,
    it gently clear'd my way,
And through the pleasing snares of vice,
    more to be fear'd than they.

8 When worn with sickness, oft hast thou
    with health renew'd my face;
And when in sins and sorrows sunk,
    reviv'd my soul with grace.

9 Thy bounteous hand with worldly bliss
    has made my cup run o'er;
And in a kind and faithful friend
    has doubled all my store.

10 Ten thousand thousand precious gifts
    my daily thanks employ;
Nor is the least a chearful heart,
    that tastes those gifts with joy.

11 Through ev'ry period of my life
    thy goodness I'll pursue;
And after death, in distant worlds,
    the glorious theme renew.
12 When nature fails, and day and night
    divide thy works no more,
My ever grateful heart, O Lord,
    thy mercy shall adore.
13 Through all eternity to thee
    a joyful song I'll raise;
For oh! eternity's too short
    to utter all thy praise.

HYMN XV.

On the GLORY *of* GOD *in the Starry Heavens: Being a Translation of Part of the 19th Psalm of David.*

1 THE spacious firmament on high,
    With all the blue etherial sky,
And spangled heav'ns, a shining frame,
    Their great original proclaim.
2 Th' unwearied sun from day to day,
    Does his Creator's pow'r display,
And publishes to ev'ry land
    The work of an Almighty Hand.
3 Soon as the ev'ning shades prevail,
    The moon takes up the wond'rous tale;
And nightly, to the list'ning earth,
    Repeats the story of her birth;
4 Whilst all the stars that round her burn,
    And all the planets in their turn,
Confirm the tidings as they roll,
    And spread the truth from pole to pole.
5 What though in solemn silence all
    Move round the dark terrestrial ball;
What though no real voice nor sound
    Amidst their radiant orbs be found;
6 In reason's ear they all rejoice,
    And utter forth a glorious voice,
For ever singing as they shine,
    "The Hand that made us is Divine."

HYMN XVI.

On the Providence of GOD: *Taken chiefly from the 23d Psalm of David.*

1 THE Lord my pasture shall prepare,
    And feed me with a shepherd's care;
His presence shall my wants supply,
    And guard me with a watchful eye;
2 My noon-day walks he shall attend,
    And all my midnight hours defend:

    When in the sultry glebe I faint,
    Or on the thirsty mountain pant,
3 To fertile vales and dewy meads
    My weary wand'ring steps he leads,
    Where peaceful rivers, soft and slow,
    Amid the verdant landskip flow.
4 Though in the paths of death I tread,
    With gloomy horrors overspread;
    My stedfast heart shall fear no ill,
    For thou, O Lord, art with me still;
5 Thy friendly crook shall give me aid,
    And guide me through the dreadful shade:
    Though in a bare and rugged way,
    Through devious lonely wilds I stray,
6 Thy bounty shall my pains beguile,
    The barren wilderness shall smile,
    With sudden greens and herbage crown'd,
    And streams shall murmur all around.

HYMN XVII.
For the Mercies of Redemption.

1 ALL-glorious God, what hymns of praise
    Shall our transported voices raise!
    What ardent love and zeal are due,
    While heav'n stands open to our view!
2 Once we were fall'n, and O how low!
    Just on the brink of endless woe;
    When Jesus, from the realms above,
    Borne on the wings of boundless love,
3 Scatter'd the shades of death and night,
    And spread around his heav'nly light!
    By him what wond'rous grace is shown
    To souls impoverish'd and undone.
4 He shows, beyond these mortal shores,
    A bright inheritance as ours;
    Where Saints in light our coming wait,
    To share their holy, happy state!

HYMN XVIII.
For public Mercies and Deliverances.

1 SAlvation doth to God belong;
    His pow'r and grace shall be our song;
    From him alone all mercies flow;
    His arm alone subdues the foe!
2 Then praise this God, who bows his ear
    Propitious to his people's pray'r;
    And though deliv'rance he may stay,
    Yet answers still in his own day.
3 O may this goodness lead our land,
    Still sav'd by thine Almighty hand,

The tribute of its love to bring
To thee, our Saviour and our King;
4 Till ev'ry public temple raise
A song of triumph to thy praise;
And ev'ry peaceful private home
To thee a temple shall become.
5 Still be it our supreme delight,
To walk as in thy glorious sight;
Still in thy precepts and thy fear,
Till life's last hour, to persevere.

HYMN XIX.
On GOD's Dominion over the Sea.

1 GOD of the seas! thine awful voice
Bids all the rolling waves rejoice!
And one soft word of thy command
Can sink them silent in the sand.
2 The smallest fish that swims the seas,
Sportful, to thee a tribute pays;
And largest monsters of the deep,
At thy command, or rage or sleep.
3 Thus is thy glorious pow'r ador'd
Among the wat'ry nations, Lord!
Yet men, who trace the dang'rous waves,
Forget the Mighty God who saves!

HYMN XX.
Which may be used at Sea or on Land.

1 LORD! for the just thou dost provide;
thou art their sure defence!
Eternal Wisdom is their guide,
their help Omnipotence.
2 Though they through foreign lands should roam,
and breathe the tainted air
In burning climates, far from home;
yet thou, their God, art there.
3 Thy goodness sweetens ev'ry soil,
makes ev'ry country please;
Thou on the snowy hills dost smile,
and smooth'st the rugged seas!
4 When waves on waves, to heav'n uprear'd,
defy'd the pilot's art;
When terror in each face appear'd,
and sorrow in each heart;
5 To thee I rais'd my humble pray'r,
to snatch me from the grave!
I found thine ear not slow to hear,
nor short thine arm to save!
6 Thou gav'st the word—the winds did cease,
the storms obey'd thy will,

The raging sea was hush'd in peace,
  and ev'ry wave was still!
7 For this, my life, in ev'ry state,
  a life of praise shall be;
And death, when death shall be my fate,
  shall join my soul to thee.

HYMN XXI.
Prayer and Hope of VICTORY.

1 NOW may the God of grace and pow'r
    attend his people's humble cry;
  Defend them in the needful hour,
    and send deliv'rance from on high.
2 In his salvation is our hope,
    and in the Name of Israel's God
  Our troops shall lift their banners up;
    our navies spread their flags abroad.
3 Some trust in horses train'd for war,
    and some of chariots make their boasts;
  Our surest expectations are
    from thee, the Lord of heav'nly hosts!
4 Then save us, Lord, from slavish fear,
    and let our trust be firm and strong,
  Till thy salvation shall appear,
    and hymns of peace conclude our song.

HYMN XXII.
For the use of the SICK.

1 WHEN dangers, woes, or death are nigh,
    Past mercies teach me where to fly;
  Thine arm, Almighty God, can aid,
  When sickness grieves, and pains invade.
2 To all the various helps of art
  Kindly thy healing pow'r impart;
  Bethesda's* bath refus'd to save
  Unless an Angel bless'd the wave.
3 All med'cines act by thy decree,
  Receive commission all from thee;
  And not a plant which spreads the plains,
  But teems with health, when heav'n ordains.
4 Clay and Siloam's† pool, we find,
  At heav'n's command restor'd the blind;
  And Jordan's‡ waters hence were seen
  To wash a Syrian leper clean.
5 But grant me nobler favours still,
  Grant me to know and do thy will;
  Purge my foul soul from ev'ry stain,
  And save me from eternal pain.

* *John* v. 4.   † *John* ix. 7.   ‡ *Kings* v. 10.

6 Can such a wretch for pardon sue?
   My crimes, my crimes, arise in view,
   Arrest my trembling tongue in pray'r,
   And pour the horrors of despair.
7 But thou, regard my contrite sighs,
   My tortur'd breast, my streaming eyes;
   To me thy boundless love extend,
   My God, my Father, and my Friend.
8 These lovely Names I ne'er could plead,
   Had not thy Son vouchsaf'd to bleed;
   His Blood procures for human race
   Admittance to the Throne of Grace.
9 When sin has shot its poison'd dart,
   And conscious guilt corrodes the heart,
   His blood is all sufficient found
   To draw the shaft, and heal the wound.
10 What arrows pierce so deep as sin?
   What venom gives such pain within?
   Thou great Physician of the soul,
   Rebuke my pangs, and make me whole.
11 O! if I trust thy sov'reign skill,
   And bow submissive to thy will,
   Sickness and death shall both agree
   To bring me, Lord, at last to thee.

HYMN XXIII.

On Recovery from Sickness;

1 WHEN we are rais'd from deep distress,
    our God deserves our song;
  We take the pattern of our praise
    from Hezekiah's‡ tongue.
2 The gates of the devouring grave
    are open'd wide in vain,
  If he that holds the keys of death
    command them fast again.
3 When he but speaks the healing word,
    then no disease withstands;
  Fevers and plagues obey the Lord,
    and fly, as he commands.
4 If half the strings of life should break,
    he can our frame restore,
  And cast our sins behind his back,
    and they are found no more.
5 To him I cry'd---"Thy servant save,
    "thou ever good and just;
  "Thy pow'r can rescue from the grave;
    "thy pow'r is all my trust!"

‡ *Isaiah* xxxix. 9, &c.

6 He heard, and sav'd my soul from death,
   and dry'd my falling tears;
Now to his praise I'll spend my breath,
   through my remaining years.

HYMN XXIV.
On the same.

1 MY God, since thou hast rais'd me up,
     thee I'll extol with thankful voice;
   Restor'd by thine Almighty pow'r,
     with fear before thee I'll rejoice.
2 With troubles worn, with pain oppress'd,
     to thee I cry'd, and thou did'st save;
   Thou did'st support my sinking hopes,
     my life did'st rescue from the grave.
3 Wherefore, ye Saints! rejoice with me,
     with me sing praises to the Lord;
   Call all his goodness to your mind,
     and all his faithfulness record.
4 His anger is but short; his love
     which is our life, hath certain stay;
   Grief may continue for a night,
     but joy returns with rising day!
5 Then what I vow'd in my distress,
     in happier hours I now will give,
   And strive, that in my grateful verse
     his praises may for ever live.
6 To Father, Son, and Holy Ghost,
     the blest and undivided Three,
   The one sole Giver of all life,
     glory and praise for ever be.

HYMN XXV.
FUNERAL CONSOLATIONS.

1 HEAR what the voice from heav'n declares
     to those in Christ who die!
   "Releas'd from all their earthly cares,
   " they reign with him on high."
2 Then, why lament departed friends,
     or shake at death's alarms?
   Death's but the servant Jesus sends
     to call us to his arms.
3 If sin be pardon'd we're secure,
     death hath no sting beside;
   The law gave sin its strength and pow'r;
     but Christ, our ransom, died!
4 The graves of all his saints he bless'd,
     when in the grave he lay;
   And rising thence, their hopes he rais'd
     to everlasting day!

5 Then joyfully, while life we have,
   to Christ, our life, we'll sing—
  "Where is thy victory, O grave?
  "and where, O death, thy sting?"

HYMN XXVI.

CHRIST's Commission to preach the GOSPEL.
St. Matth. *Chap.* x.

1 GO forth, ye Heralds, in my Name,
   sweetly the Gospel trumpet sound;
  The glorious Jubilee proclaim,
   where'er the human race is found.

2 The joyful news to all impart,
   and teach them where salvation lies;
  With care bind up the broken heart,
   and wipe the tears from weeping eyes.

3 Be wise as serpents where you go,
   but harmless as the peaceful dove,
  And let your heav'n-taught conduct show
   that ye're commission'd from above.

4 Freely from me ye have receiv'd,
   freely, in love, to others give;
  Thus shall your doctrines be believ'd,
   and, by your labours, sinners live.

HYMN XXVII.

The same COMMISSION, *from St.* Mark xvi. 15, &c. *and
from St.* Matth. xxviii. 18, &c.

1 "GO preach my Gospel, saith the Lord,
   "bid the whole earth my grace receive;
  "Explain to them my sacred Word,
   "bid them believe, obey, and live!

2 "I'll make my great commission known,
   "and ye shall prove my Gospel true,
  "By all the works that I have done,
   "and all the wonders ye shall do.

3 "Go heal the sick, go raise the dead,
   "go cast out devils in my Name;
  "Nor let my Prophets be afraid,
   "though Greeks reproach, and Jews blaspheme.

4 "While thus ye follow my commands,
   "I'm with you till the world shall end;
  "All pow'r is trusted in my hands;
   "I can destroy, and can defend."

5 He spake, and light shone round his head;
   on a bright cloud to heav'n he rode!
  They to the farthest nations spread
   the grace of their ascended God.

The END.

An Alphabetical TABLE,

Showing where to find each PSALM or HYMN by its Beginning.

PSALMS.

A	Page		Page
AGainst all those	40	Just Judge of heav'n,	52
As pants the Hart	51	I waited meekly	49
At length, by certain	87	**L**	
B		Let all the just	38
Behold, O God	98	Let all the lands,	76
Bless God, my soul	127	Let all the list'ning	58
Bless God, ye servants,	171	Let David, Lord,	170
D		Let God, the God	77
Defend me, Lord,	35	Lord, hear my cry,	71
Deliver me, O Lord,	69	Lord, hear my pray'r,	180
Do thou, O God,	66	Lord, hear the voice	6
F		Lord, hear the voice	74
For ever bless'd	181	Lord, let thy just	85
For thee, O God,	75	Lord, not to us,	145
From lowest depths	169	Lord, save me, for	64
From my youth	168	Lord, thou hast	106
G		Lord, who's the happy	15
Give ear, thou Judge	65	**M**	
God in the great	102	My crafty foe, with	43
God is our refuge	56	My God, my God,	25
God's temple crowns	108	My soul for help	72
H		My soul, inspir'd	125
Had not the Lord,	166	My soul with grateful	146
Happy the man	50	**N**	
Have mercy, Lord,	61	No change of time	18
Hear, O my people;	93	**O**	
He's blest whose sins	37	O all ye people,	57
He that has God	114	O come, loud anthems	118
How good and	115	O God, my gracious	73
Hold not thy peace,	103	O God, my heart	138
How bless'd are they,	149	O God, whose former	139
How blest is he,	3	O God of Hosts,	104
How long wilt	14	O God, to whom	116
How many, Lord,	4	O God, who hast	71
How vast must	171	O Israel's Shepherd,	99
I		O Lord, I am not	169
Jehovah reigns,	120	O Lord my God,	7
Jehovah reigns;	121	O Lord, my rock,	32
I'll celebrate thy	34	O Lord, our fathers	53
In deep distress	164	O Lord, the Saviour	113
In Judah the	91	O Lord, that art my	5
In thee I put	83	O Lord, to my	83
In vain, O man	63	Of mercy's never	123
Judge me, O Lord,	30	On thee, who dwell'st	166

	Page		Page
O praise the Lord, and	183	Thy chast'ning wrath,	47
O praise the Lord, for	147	Thy dreadful anger,	6
O praise the Lord in	188	Thy mercies, Lord,	109
O praise the Lord with	184	Thy mercy, Lord,	67
O praise the Lord with	171	Thy presence why	11
O praise ye the Lord,	187	Through all the	39
O render thanks,	129	To bless thy chosen	77
O render thanks to	132	To celebrate thy	9
O Thou, to whom all	8	To God I cry'd,	92
O 'Twas a joyful	165	To God, in whom	29
		To God, our never	101
P		To God the mighty	173
Praise ye the Lord;	142	To God, with	179
Preserve me, Lord,	177	To God your grateful	135
Protect me from my	15	To my complaint,	106
R		To my just plea	16
Resolv'd to watch	48	To thee, my God	108
S		To thee, O God,	90
Save me, O God,	80	To thee, O Lord,	178
Since godly men	13	To Sion's hill	165
Since I have plac'd	12	**W**	
Sing to the Lord	119	We build with	167
Sing to the Lord	121	When I pour out	123
Speak, O ye judges	68	When Israel by	144
Sure wicked fools	14	When Sion's God	167
T		Who place on Sion's	166
That man is blest	143	When we, our	174
Thee I will bless,	182	With my whole	175
The Heav'ns declare	22	While I the King's	55
The king, O Lord,	24	Whom should I fear,	31
The Lord hath spoke,	60	Why hast thou cast	88
The Lord himself,	27	With chearful notes	147
The spacious earth	28	With glory clad,	116
The Lord, the only	57	With one consent,	122
The Lord to thy	23	With restless and	3
The Lord unto my Lord	142	**Y**	
The man is blest that	168		
The wicked fools	64	Ye boundless realms	186
Though wicked men	44	Ye princes, that	33
Thou, Lord, my	176	Ye saints and servants	144

HYMNS

The TABLE.

HYMNS.

	Page
A	
ALL-glorious God, what hymns of praise	199
And are we now brought near to God,	194
C	
Christ from the dead is rais'd, and made	192
Come, Holy Ghost! Creator, come,	ib.
Come, Holy Spirit, heav'nly Dove,	193
F	
From whence these direful omens round,	191
G	
God of the seas! thine awful voice	200
Go forth, ye Heralds, in my Name,	204
Go preach my Gospel, saith the Lord,	ib.
H	
Hear what the voice from heav'n declares	203
He's come! let ev'ry knee be bent,	193
L	
Lord! for the just thou dost provide;	200
M	
My God, and is thy Table spread?	194
My God, since thou hast rais'd me up,	203
N	
Now may the God of grace and pow'r	201
S	
Salvation doth to God belong;	199
Since Christ our Passover is slain,	191
T	
The God of life, whose constant care	195
The Lord my pasture shall prepare,	198
The spacious firmament on high,	ib.
Thou, God, all glory, honour, pow'r,	193
W	
When all thy mercies, O my God,	197
When dangers, woes, or death are nigh,	201
When, rising from the bed of death,	196
When we are rais'd from deep distress,	202
While Angels thus, O Lord, rejoice,	190
While shepherds watch'd their flocks by night,	ib.

www.ingramcontent.com/pod-product-compliance
Lightning Source LLC
Chambersburg PA
CBHW020911230426
43666CB00008B/1415